The Anti Obama Book - The Straight Facts As To Why Obama Sucks

By David Nordmark

Also By David Nordmark

Understanding American Exceptionalism

Thank-you for downloading my book. Please REVIEW my book on Amazon. I appreciate your feedback so that I can make the next version even better. Thank-you so much!

Table of Contents

Obama and the Media

Despite a record that included chronic high-unemployment, record deficits and debt, fiasco's as large as his stimulus program and as "small" (hey, it was only 500 million dollars) as Solyndra, despite not delivering on his promises of above it all bi-partisanship while demonstrating almost no leadership skills in the White House, Barack Hussein Obama was re-elected to a second term as President of the United States on November 6, 2012. How was this alchemy accomplished?

In one word, the media.

Although their power is waning and their balance sheets are often (deservedly) bleeding red, the mainstream media in America still have a tremendous power to set the terms of the debate, the over-arching narrative, and whether an issue even sees the light day or is allowed to be snuffed out due to lack of oxygen. Make no mistake about it; to the vast majority of the non-Fox media, President Obama is their guy. From the beginning they've promoted him, ran interference for him, lied for him, and have viciously targeted anyone who might threaten him.

What is the source of this, often unreciprocated, media love? I suspect the main reason is because, in Obama, the media have found almost their perfect surrogate. When they look at Obama it's almost like they're looking at themselves. What's not to love? He's a man of the left. So are they. He fancies himself an intellectual and the smartest man in the room. So do they. He pronounces himself a post-partisan "uniter" in rhetoric, while taking a my-way-or-the-highway approach in action. He's a left-winger who fights back! What's more, he's black (but not too black). Forget all of that malarkey about being judged by the content of your character rather than the color of your skin. For the mostly white liberal media Obama allows them to massage their liberal guilt while simultaneously allowing them to feel good about themselves. How could they not love him?

This is why neither scandals nor Obama's dismal record have been able to diminish him. If you doubt this for a second compare the media responses to Hurricane Katrina back in 2005 under the hated George W. Bush to their kid glove treatment of Obama with Sandy. During the former Bush was pilloried continually for being allegedly uncaring and incompetent while with Sandy Obama was allowed to walk around in a bomber jacket for a day and the story was dropped. Or compare the doggedness and relentless time and effort the press spent on the Valerie Plame non-story (they even made a movie about it!) vs. the bordering on criminal disinterest the press has shown during the Benghazi terrorist attack. Former Democratic Pollster Pat Caddell has stated that with this performance the mainstream media has crossed a line and become an enemy of the American people. The press often bemoaned the fact that former President Reagan seemed to wear Teflon as controversies just never stuck to him. Some have said the same of Obama, but it just isn't true. Why do you need Teflon when you have a press willing and eager to sacrifice their last vestiges of credibility to take a bullet for you? It's actually too bad. If Obama had protected the Libyan compound with the same ferociousness that the media guard him, Ambassador Stevens would likely still be alive today. As it is they show no interest in the circumstances or the Obama administrations constantly changing story related to the Libyan deaths. They know whom they want to protect, and it isn't the American people or the truth. Not if it in anyway endangers their chosen one.

And in the end they accomplished their goal. Mitt Romney has been vanquished and their guy is back in the White House. What will the next 4 years look like? One thing for sure is that Obama himself hasn't changed at all. As I write this all of the worst qualities of the President are on display as America moves towards the "Fiscal Cliff". The only proposal Obama has put forward is to raise taxes on job creators, or what he calls 'The Rich". By doing so he will raise enough money to fund the federal government for an extra 8 days. Just as he failed to do in his first term he has not put forward any plan for spending cuts or entitlement reform. If he were anything like the image the media have created Obama should be working around the clock to come up with some sort of compromise. Instead, as he has always done in the past, he is attempting to hover above it all by giving campaign style speeches when he isn't hitting the links. Obama may be a master at getting elected (although I'd like to see how he'd do without his media palace guards) but he isn't a leader. All he knows how to do is to spend money America doesn't have. He is what he is, and we're stuck with him.

How can we expect the media to behave during Obama's second term? If you guessed that not much has changed here either, you're right. In an effort to shore up their tattered credibility they will offer up some token criticism from time to time. However, Obama is still their guy, and any story that might impinge on their desire for him to be declared the greatest president ever will be minimized at best and ignored at worst. Again, you are seeing this play out in how they are covering the fiscal cliff. While Rome burns and Obama plays golf, the media are putting no pressure on him to present a credible plan to deal with the immense financial challenges America is now facing. As it is for Obama's lack of leadership on the financial crises, so it will be for the coming tab on Obamacare or his failures in the Middle East. The media are willing to stand by their man and parrot whatever talking points the Obama White House wishes them too. Remember what Pat Caddell said. The press can now be viewed as the enemy of the American people. Never forget that.

The media are determined to drag Obama into the ranks of successful presidents, no matter how unworthy he is. Any story that can be contorted to advance the narrative that Obama is a great, wise, post-partisan healer of the nation's wounds will be advanced. Any that do not will be minimized and ignored. As stomach churning as this process will be to watch, it will only get worse when he leaves office and discussion of his "legacy" begins. That's where this book comes in.

The truth is that Obama has never been a reach across the isle can't we all get along kind of guy. He is a bitter, partisan hack who has risen to his station in life through the black arts of self-promotion and a media who are willing to cover for him. The proof of that is in his actual record. The media will try and scrub it clean but they cannot be allowed to succeed. This book will cover the real Obama's record, and it isn't pretty. When viewed through clear lenses, as opposed to the media created fog, it becomes obvious that Obama is not a great president at all. In fact, he sucks.

Obama and America

On January 20, 2009, Barack Obama was sworn in as the 44th president of the United States of America. His meteoric rise from obscurity to the nations highest office was unprecedented in American history. With America involved in two wars, still under terrorist threat, and the economy shaky, he was about to face great challenges. Would he be up to the task?

To his supporters, there was no doubt. Despite his lack of experience or any kind of track record of success (other than publishing two books about himself) Obama stood apart. He was the leader they had been waiting for and they drank deeply from his cup of hope and change. His pronouncements on being a post-partisan, non-ideological leader were eagerly latched onto by a population grown tired of the divisions represented by the later Bush years. Obama offered his supporters the mirage of being able to have their cake and eat it too. What problem did you want the new messiah to heal? Did you want the deficit eliminated, a booming economy, free health care, everyone in the world to like America? Whatever your dreams and desires Obama the candidate reflected them back to you in Technicolor. Obama, floating above it all like some sort of demi god, would be able to do all that, as well as presumably allow the lame to walk and prevent the ocean's rise. What wasn't there to like?

To his detractors, however, Obama came across as a glib, slick talker. His speeches could be nice, so long as you didn't dwell too long on what he actually said. Talking was one thing, but actually governing and getting results in the real world were something else entirely. Obama's past, his work experience, the fact that he never held a job in which he was responsible for the outcome, worried these people. In his speeches he came across as a college student who had read some books by Noam Chomsky and, untouched by real world experience, had everything figured out. He was a part time professor with no track record and no executive experience. Being president would be his first real job, and his background suggested he was woefully unprepared. Sure the media loved him, but they loved him because they reminded them of themselves. Nothing in his background suggested he was prepared for the harsh realities of the job he was about to take.

Which view was correct?

Hindsight is 20/20, but the harsh light of reality has brought the hazy reflection of Obama into sharp focus. He is not a post-partisan politician who is able to cross party lines. The reality is he has never been able to do this in the past, and he can't do it now. His sense of intellectual self-importance, that he is smarter than anyone else, is now only believed by himself and a shrinking number of media acolytes. He fundamentally doesn't understand what made America great. America needs leadership, but Obama has no desire or even idea how to provide it, much less govern. In office Obama doesn't so much govern as preside. He likes to float above it all, determined not to be held responsible for the displeasure he causes. Again and again, in decision after decision, we see how Obama's inexperience, vanity and false understanding of America have made problems worse. This is why his whole first term has mainly involved stumbling from gaffe to gaffe while he preens and wags his finger at everyone around him for seemingly letting him down.

From my observations, there are several huge gaps in Obama's cognitive toolkit that prevent him from truly understanding America or the American system. Let us now take a look at these holes in Obama's understanding, as they allow us to better understand his past and likely future failures.

American Exceptionalism

In my first book "Understanding American Exceptionalism" I attempted to explain what made America so unique in the first place. Without repeating everything in that book, here is the executive summary. (And as a bonus, just by reading this, you'll already know more than Barack Obama).

Broadly speaking, there are two ways to organize a society. One is the "French Style", or "Top Down" society. The other is the "English Style", or "Bottom Up" version.

When it comes to the question as to how best to organize a society, the French Style answer is to put its faith in a few. The theory is that a few learned souls will have the wisdom to create just laws and regulations to govern everybody. Everything is governed from the top down.

As you might expect, the English Style, or Bottom Up society, is the polar opposite. It is rooted in the concept of Natural Rights as espoused by such thinkers as John Locke. What the English figured out, and what the French keep missing, is that the simplest, least expensive, most effective way to build a virtuous society is to see each individual as a moral agent, either adding or subtracting from the fabric of society. In such a society the goal of a government is not to control or manage people. Rather, it is to foster an environment in which each individual, subject to the same rules, will control him or her self. The English Style ultimately believes that sovereignty, the power to act, is best left to the individual citizen.

Former British Prime Minister Margret Thatcher once said, *"Europe was created by history. America was created by philosophy"*. When America's founders met in Philadelphia that is exactly what they did. They embraced these English ideas and took them further than even the mother country was willing to go. This is what made America so exceptional. By design, it put as much sovereignty as possible in the hands of the individual citizen. It is free citizens that make America America, not this or that government program. I do not believe that Barack Obama understands this.

Citizens vs. Subjects

English-style societies, by reserving the maximum amount of decision making with the people, tend to produce energetic, dynamic, citizens. By citizens, I mean individuals who exhibit a high degree of personal responsibility and initiative. Citizens take it upon themselves to get things done. They don't wait for anyone else, much less the government. Friedrich Hayek, writing in *"The Road to Serfdom"*, nicely encapsulated the characteristics that make up a true citizen:

> *The virtues possessed by Anglo-Saxons in a higher degree than most other people, excepting only a few of the smaller nations, like the Swiss and the Dutch, were independence and self-reliance, individual initiative and local responsibility, the successful reliance on voluntary activity, noninterference with one's neighbor and tolerance of the different and queer, respect for custom and tradition, and a healthy suspicion of power and authority.*

To put it another way, English style societies produce adults. What does it mean to be an adult? My understanding is that you become an adult when you accept the responsibilities of life and look after yourself. You don't depend on your parents anymore. You have the power to do what you want, but you also accept the responsibility that comes along with it. Top-down French-style societies, by reserving true power for an anointed elite, do not produce citizens or adults of this kind. Rather, they tend to engender servile subjects, people who are all too willing to take their marching orders from the sovereign and constantly look to him to do things they should be doing for themselves. Countries like Greece are perfect examples of societies that are now made up of too many subjects. When the bankrupt government tries to pull back, subjects react like spoiled children. The Occupy movement is largely made up of subjects.

Obama either does not understand this, or understands it so well that he wants to create as many subjects as possible. I remember Obama praising a girl who had written him, asking that he and the Congress provide the funds to help paint her school. This is a perfect example of the subject mentality. How hard would it be to organize some volunteers to paint the school? How much cheaper would it be to do it this way, as opposed to beseeching good King Barack to do it for her? Which way is truly the American way? Obama's entire "career" as a community organizer involved organizing subjects to agitate people against their fellow citizens and the state. When Barack Obama attempts to praise America, he typically does it by praising actions that were attained via government. This is a perversion of American exceptionalism and the American idea, but Obama seems to have no conception of this.

Consequential Knowledge

"We don't know a millionth of one percent about anything." - Thomas Edison

"We can create millions of jobs, starting with a 21st century economic recovery plan that

puts Americans to work building wind farms, solar panels, and fuel-efficient cars. We can spark the dynamism of our economy [by investing in] renewable energy that will give life to new businesses and industries with good jobs that pay well and can't be outsourced." – Obama, speaking on his economic plans in 2008

Another major advantage of the English style system over its French counterpart is the way it can harness the broad knowledge that exists within a society. In any country, but particularly one as large as the United States, the sheer volume of knowledge and experience held by the citizenry is mind blowing. However, that enormous wealth of knowledge is obviously diffuse. It is spread out. It is not concentrated in any one man or woman. Even if Obama were the smartest man in America (which I highly doubt), does he know more than the rest of the population combined?

How does this work? By leaving consequential decisions in the hands of citizens and utilizing the price system, a tremendous amount of information is relayed. Let's say you want to build a bridge, but you don't take into account what anything costs. What materials do you use? Do you build the bridge out of gold? It would certainly look pretty, but gold is fairly soft. Maybe you should use diamonds, which are one of the hardest substances on Earth? Steel, wood, stone, plastics, metals, there are so many choices. How do you make an intelligent choice?

When prices are added into the mix, however, things become much clearer. Diamonds are very expensive, and are best used in jewelry and other limited industrial uses. This is the information prices effortlessly transmit. This is Adam Smith's famous "invisible hand". Prices allow everyone in the economy to transmit information about how to best put to use limited resources. This is why we build bridges out of steel and not some other material.

Matt Ridley, author or *"The Rational Optimist: How Prosperity Evolves"*, puts it this way:

Brilliant people, be they anthropologists, psychologists or economists, assume that brilliance is the key to human achievement. They vote for the cleverest people to run governments, they ask the cleverest experts to devise plans for the economy, they credit the cleverest scientists with discoveries, and they speculate on how human intelligence evolved in the first place.
They are all barking up the wrong tree. The key to human achievement is not individual intelligence at all....The reason some economies work better than others is certainly not because they have cleverer people in charge, and the reason some places make great discoveries is not because they have smarter people.
Human achievement is entirely a networking phenomenon. It is by putting brains together through the division of labor — through trade and specialization — that human society stumbled upon a way to raise the living standards, carrying capacity, technological

17

virtuosity and knowledge base of the species. We can see this in all sorts of phenomena: the correlation between technology and connected population size in Pacific islands; the collapse of technology in people who became isolated, like native Tasmanians; the success of trading city states in Greece, Italy, Holland and south-east Asia; the creative consequences of trade. Human achievement is based on collective intelligence — the nodes in the human neural network are people themselves. By each doing one thing and getting good at it, then sharing and combining the results through exchange, people become capable of doing things they do not even understand. As the economist Leonard Read observed in his essay "I, Pencil' (which I'd like everybody to read), no single person knows how to make even a pencil — the knowledge is distributed in society among many thousands of graphite miners, lumberjacks, designers and factory workers. That's why, as Friedrich Hayek observed, central planning never worked: the cleverest person is no match for the collective brain at working out how to distribute consumer goods....

(Note: I've included Read's essay as an appendix to the end of this book)

The bottom up system combined with prices allows people to act like processors in a massively parallel computer. Compare how powerful this bottom up computer is to the top down computer, which relies on only a few processors to make decisions. It is this massive knowledge-processing gap that prevents a few people, no matter how elite they are, from a running a country effectively.

President Obama, through his speeches and actions, demonstrates that he has no conception of this. When he praises high-speed rail as something money should be spent on, how does he know this? If high-speed rail were so great, why hasn't private industry already built it? These questions don't seem to darken his self-assured thoughts and pretty but vacuous speeches, but the reason is obvious. People are not willing to spend enough of their hard earned money to make high-speed rail profitable. The "bottom up computer" is saying loudly that people want to spend their money elsewhere. They'd rather buy a car, take a bus or taxi, bike, etc. Top down politicians like Obama love to make grand pronouncements and be seen with what is considered a sexy new technology. However, they aren't willing to invest their own money in it. Nor do they bear any responsibility later when the ribbons have been cut and the marching bands have gone home and it turns out your fancy high speed rail system is losing money hand over fist. This has been the experience the world over, particularly China, which Obama has often wistfully pointed out would be so much easier to rule.

Obama often talks about the need for investments (his code word for more government spending). We need to invest in the future! But how does he know what the smart investments are? He is happy to invest in solar panel companies like Solyndra, for example. But where does he get the money to invest in it? The only thing he can do is to take money out of the private sector. Every dollar that goes into a Solyndra, high speed rail, or similar government approved endeavor is one less dollar that someone in the private sector has to produce a new good or service.

Reread the Edison and Obama quotes that began this section. Why is Edison, with so many great accomplishments, so humble about his knowledge as compared to Obama, the man with none? The answer is that reality tempers you; it beats you up and knocks your grand visions to the ground. Only when you start respecting reality do you make any progress. In Edison's case, when you know it took more than a thousand tries to make a basic light bulb, you are going to be much less prone to making sweeping statements about changing the world, transforming America or stopping the sea levels from rising. This is what always concerned me about Obama when I listened to his speeches. He always came across as a know-it-all college student. When it's only words and you haven't ever really been tested by reality, anything must seem possible. All you need to do is say it, and everything is going to fall into line. As Ed Klein put it in his book *"The Amateur"*, Obama:

> *"...didn't know what he didn't know"*

For such a man to occupy the most powerful position in the world is a terrifying thought. That he has been re-elected is a testament to the skill of his campaign staff and the obsequiousness of the media.

Where Do Jobs Come From?

Finally, I'm also convinced that Obama has no idea how wealth or jobs are created in an economy. Do you know where they come from? It's OK if you don't. Many famous economists, like the New York Times' Paul Krugman, have no idea either. In order to explore this topic, let's do a little thought experiment.

Imagine an island on which there are only two inhabitants, Chuck and Bob. In this economy, there are no jobs, so the unemployment rate is 100%. Now imagine that you're Obama. How do you fix this?

Obama can't create any jobs, as the government has no money of its own. The only thing a government can do is collect money from taxes. However, in this economy no one is working, and there is no money to tax.

Let's say that Obama is able to borrow some money from another island. He then uses this money to create some jobs. Perhaps he hires Chuck to sweep the beach, and Bob to regulate this activity. This appears to work in the short term. Both Chuck and Bob are nominally employed, at least. However, at some point, the money runs out and we're back to the same situation as before, except it's worse. The unemployment rate is once again at 100% and Obama has created a debt.

So what's the solution?

The answer, it turns out, doesn't originate with Obama at all. It's up to Chuck and Bob.

Perhaps Chuck has a skill at weaving baskets, whereas Bob is good at fishing. They both get to work, and now real wealth is being created. Chuck and Bob can trade amongst themselves, or they can sell their wares to other islands. The key point here is to understand just what the wellspring of wealth and jobs truly is. It does NOT come from top down actions of the government. It comes from individual human action. Or, to put it another way:

A job is created when a person creates, or helps to create, a good or service that someone else is voluntarily willing to pay for.

If we begin to add people to our simple economy it then makes sense for Obama to tax the individuals on the island so that he can then hire some needed public employees, like policeman or fireman. However, it must always be remembered that although this is important work, these government jobs are not wealth creating jobs. Rather, they help to support the wealth creators, in this case by protecting them from theft and the threat of fire.

A problem occurs when people confuse wealth creating private sector jobs with the wealth supporting ones that exist in the public sector. Growing the public sector is not an economic program. If it grows too much the accompanying taxes and regulations are likely to expand as well. If they grow too large they may reach a point where the Chuck and Bob's of the world stop doing their thing. Wealth ceases to be created and the economy begins to decline. If you want to see an example of this process in action, look at Detroit – one of many places in America whose history is literally a case study in private-sector glory being snuffed out by government growth.

From his background and pronouncements, most famously his *"You didn't build that"* speech, I do not believe that Obama understands this.

This concludes our look at the major gaps that I suspect exist within Obama's intellectual framework. As we begin to go through the examples of why Obama sucks, you will see how these blind spots lead Obama to make the wrong decisions time and again.

Reason #26 That Obama Sucks - Cash for Clunkers

"I think it's the worst thing we've ever done," – Jerry Frazier, owner of Save-A-Lot Motors

Cash for Clunkers was one of the first economic initiatives of the Obama administration. Although small in scale (it "only" cost around 3 billion dollars) it proved to be an accurate template for many of the policies that would follow. All of the elements that would define later Obama initiatives are here. An unwarranted belief in government top down thinking, badly managed from the beginning, and done with no conception of what the unintended consequences might be. It stands as a case study in how politicians only see the short-term consequences of their actions. However, it is the long term and unseen consequences that we must focus on to judge the benefits of any given policy. When seen through these lenses, Cash for Clunkers was a disaster, both in its outcomes and how it became the template that the economically illiterate Obama would use in the future.

The idea behind the program was that the federal government would give people a rebate of between $3500 and $4500 to trade in their old gas guzzling cars. The trade in car had to get less than 18 miles per gallon, whereas the new car had to get 22 miles per gallon or more. The old "clunkers" would then be destroyed. In theory, this would cut carbon emissions and give the auto industry a boost. As with all government plans, I'm sure it probably looked good on paper and, what's more, in the short term, it seemed to work. Americans rushed into showrooms to take advantage of the program. So much so that the billion dollars allocated for the program was used up within days and Congress had to pony up an additional 2 billion to keep the program solvent. Obama Transportation Secretary Ray LaHood bragged about the seemingly early success of the program:

"Manufacturing plants have added shifts and recalled workers. Moribund showrooms were brought back to life, and consumers bought fuel-efficient cars that will save them money and improve the environment. American consumers and workers were the clear winners thanks to the Cash for Clunkers program."

But were they?

What LaHood is commenting on is, as always, the short term and seen results. What might be some of the long term and unseen consequences that he and President Obama are apparently blind to? Consider the following:

1. Programs like this simply take money away from other, less politically exciting uses. Government has no money of its own and it does not create wealth. It can only take money from one use to be spent somewhere else. In this case, if the

3 billion dollars had remained in the public sphere, how many roads could have been paved? How many teachers hired? If the money had been left in the private sector, what else might people have spent that money on? Instead of buying a new car, perhaps they'd have bought a new television or washing machine. Maybe they have gone on a vacation. Who knows? But however you look at it, whatever the seen benefits occurred from this mini "stimulus" had to be taken away from somewhere else.

2. The boom in car sales is entirely artificial. If you were thinking about getting a new car, perhaps you would wait until you could take advantage of this program. Or perhaps you'd move up your planned purchase. Either way, the overall volume of cars sold will not be changed for the year. A program such as this will only artificially create a boom, and then sales will continue as they had. This is what the chart below shows:

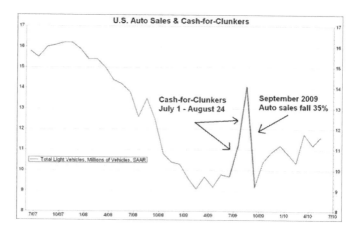

3. It hurts the poor and those who deal with used cars. A third unseen consequence of this program that Ray LaHood seems utterly unaware of is how it effects used car salesman and the poor. The old cars that were destroyed were perfectly functional. If you're a person of limited means such as a student, buying a used car may be the only option for you. However, the used car salesman can't sell you a car because the government has seen fit to destroy them in a fit of politically correct insanity. Perhaps Obama and LaHood do not understand this, but not everyone can afford a Prius.

4. It likely will not help very much to reduce carbon. For the sake of argument, let's say that reducing carbon emissions is a worthwhile goal. If so, was that the result of this program? As with so many top down schemes, what central planners miss is that people change their behavior as a result of incentives. I once had a friend who drove a used, V-8 Camaro. It was such a gasoline hog that he only drove it when he absolutely had to. What would have happened if he had been able to replace this car with a more fuel efficient one? If you guessed less bus riding and more driving, you're right.

5. It could actually increase the amount of gasoline consumed. Consider this scenario. A family owns two cars. One is

a 5-year-old Passat that gets 27mpg. The other is a gas guzzling pickup that is rarely driven. Thanks to Cash for Clunkers, the family replaces the pickup with a brand new Toyota Camry that only gets 23 mpg. The Camry now gets the majority of the use while the Passat sits idle. How does this help anyone?

6. Like most government programs, Cash for Clunkers was badly managed from the beginning. Even if the effects of the Clunkers program had been desirable, it could have been had for much cheaper. This is demonstrated by the fact that there was such a rush to take advantage of the $3500 to $4500 dollar rebate. Let's say you put your house on the market and you immediately get 10 offers. What does this tell you? Probably that your asking price is too low. In the Cash for Clunkers case, it shows that the amount offered was probably too high. Oh well. It's only (your) money.

In the end, Cash for Clunkers proved to be an eerie foreshadowing for every big government program that Obama and his team would follow in the future. Public money was wasted on a program that may have looked good on paper, but fell apart completely when it was applied to the real world.

For demonstrating his utter economic illiteracy through his championing of the Cash for Clunkers program, Barack Obama sucks.

Reason #25 That Obama Sucks - Radically Pro-Abortion

"The first thing I'd do, as president, is sign the Freedom of Choice Act. That's the first thing that I'd do." – Obama, speaking to an abortion rights group

The abortion issue is a classic example of Obama attempting to hide his radical views behind a mask of moderate words. For example, when giving the commencement address at Notre Dame University in 2009, this is what he said:

"Let's honor the conscience of those who disagree with abortion and draft a sensible conscience clause, and make sure that all of our health care policies are grounded not only in sound science, but also in clear ethics, as well as respect for the equality of women."

These soothing words were meant to calm those with pro-life views, but does he actually believe them? In order to remove this mask, as with all things Obama, it is necessary to look both at his actions and his words in unguarded moments. When viewed through these lenses it becomes obvious that not only is Obama pro-choice, but radically so. This is why his actions must be watched so closely during his second term.

First, let's look at some of his unguarded words and deeds from his past in an effort to get a clear idea of what he truly believes.

For starters, as an Illinois Senator in the year 2000, Obama opposed the Alive Infants Protection Act. This bill was designed to guarantee that non-viable infants, including those that had survived abortion procedures, would be given the same comforting care afforded to a terminally ill adult. This is not always the common practice. As Illinois registered nurse Jill Stanek testified, babies that survived abortions were often *"...taken to the Soiled Utility Room and left alone to die"*. Or, as Susan T. Muskett, legislative counsel for a pro-life group observed:

"Many of these babies lived for hours after birth, are these babies medical waste, or persons protected by the Constitution? Obama's reaction was to consider them non-entities under Roe v. Wade until they were 'viable,' even when they were gasping outside the mother."

In the House of Representatives at the federal level, a similar bill passed the House in 2001 380 to 15. Back in Illinois Obama spoke out against the federal bill and voted "present" on a similar bill. In 2002 at the federal level the same bill was brought forward, this time with a neutrality clause so that it wouldn't affect Roe vs. Wade in any way. This time it passed without any opposition and was signed into law. In 2003, a state version of the same law, with the same neutrality provision, was brought forward. Obama voted against it anyway. When forced to explain his actions Obama denied they happened and whined that his opponents were making up lies about him. However, the reality was just the opposite and his campaign was forced to back track on these statements and admit that their candidate had his legislative history wrong. As Rich Lowry put it, this episode proves that:

"Obama either didn't know his own record, or was so accustomed to shrouding it in dishonesty that it had become second nature."

Personally, my vote is with the latter.

In addition to this, Obama opposed a partial-birth abortion bill that passed both the House and Senate. Partial-birth abortion being the euphemism for the technique where the baby is pulled out feet first in order to have its brain sucked out. It's a technique that the late Democratic Senator Daniel Patrick Moynihan called *"too close to infanticide"*. Obama opposed this bill and also strongly criticized a Supreme Court decision in support of it.

In 2007 Obama, speaking before the Planned Parenthood action fund, promised that the first act he'd sign as president would be the Freedom of Choice Act. This act would not only codify Roe vs. Wade, but wipe out all current federal, state, and local restrictions on abortion that are currently enforced under Roe. This includes the Hyde amendment, which prohibits federal funding of abortion. Although he hasn't signed this act as president, it is not because he hasn't wanted to. Rather, it is because he has not been able. As he said in a press conference on April 29, 2009, although he is strongly pro-choice, the act was "*not the highest legislative priority*." Free of the need to hide his true intentions for a second term and his proven propensity for executive orders, the pro-life community must be on guard for this?

Lastly, during the 2007 campaign, Obama made a real effort to try and win over evangelicals. When asked by Pastor Rick Warren when a baby gets its rights, Obama answered blithely that the question was "*above his pay grade*". Like a con man exposed, this statement reveals Obama's utter un-seriousness on this issue. If you are willing to permit abortions under almost any circumstances, you had better consider this question, particularly if you aspire to be a serious leader.

Once in office, Obama, faced with a crumbling economy and the results of his all-out effort to pass healthcare reform, did little on the abortion front. However, this is due to the limitations of his position (you can't do everything you want to do as president, you do have to pick your priorities) and his own weak leadership skills and should not console anyone. Nonetheless, by appointing pro-choice radicals like Health and Human Services Secretary Kathleen Sebelius (who once commented, "*We are in a war*", to a pro-choice meeting), Obama has been able to put his administration on a clear and radical pro-choice path.

One of the clearest examples of this occurred when Health and Human Services (under Sebelius's leadership) chose to eliminate its grant to the US Conference of Catholic Bishops. The USCCB had been running a program that helped victims of human trafficking through programs such as employment assistance, legal services, childcare, and medical screening. However, as they are a Catholic institution, the one service they do not provide is referrals for abortion services. For this, and despite an independent board rating the USCCB program as superior to similar programs, their funding was pulled. Under the Obama administration, it is now standard procedure to deny funding to some Catholic programs based solely on their pro-life beliefs.

While this is radical enough, it pales in comparison to the Obama administration's opposition to a ban on abortions based on sex. The Prenatal Non-Discrimination Act (PRENDA) would ban abortions on the basis of gender or race, while also making the coercion of a woman to obtain a sex-based abortion illegal. As Charmaine Yoest, president of Americans United for Life, put it:

"This is a real war on women. There is nothing pro-woman about killing a baby girl because she is female, and putting her mother's health and safety at risk in the process."

There is nothing radical about this proposed bill, unless you're a radical abortionist yourself.

Hillary Clinton and many leading feminists have spoken out against abortion based on sex. Countries as diverse as Britain, Singapore, South Korea, India and even China have laws on the books opposing the practice. According to a 2006 Zogby poll, an astonishing 86 percent of Americans oppose sex-selection abortion.

And yet the Obama administration opposed the bill.

What will Obama do now that he doesn't have to worry about re-election? Time will tell, but it wouldn't surprise me if he were to attempt to pass a radical abortion bill via executive order during the waning days of his administration. This must not be allowed to happen.

For consistent opposition to any restrictions on abortion while being less than honest about his own views is yet another reason why Obama sucks.

Reason #24 That Obama Sucks - Eric Holder

*"A post-racial society is the last thing that
Holder and Obama are pursuing. "*
– economist Thomas Sowell

Despite some past actions which would give
most people pause, Eric Holder became Barack
Obama's pick as attorney general. Since then,
Holder has shown what appears to be a lack of
judgment and has involved himself and the
Justice Department in controversy after
controversy. His actions being an
embarrassment to the president
notwithstanding, Obama has stuck by his
attorney general and has refused to fire him.
This can only mean that Eric Holder's thinking
is very much in line with that of the president,
however questionable it may be.

Eric Holder first became embroiled in
controversy while acting as Deputy Attorney
General in the Clinton Administration. It was
here that he played a major role in the
pardoning of shady fugitive financier Marc
Rich. While it is true that recent presidents of
both parties have pardoned political allies who
broke the law, the Rich pardon was on an
entirely different level. This is how Debra
Saunders put it:

*"The Rich pardon broke the mold. When
Holder issued a "neutral, leaning toward"
favorable appraisal of Rich's pardon request,
he did so without a full briefing from federal*

prosecutors, in complete disregard of Rich's fugitive status and despite intelligence reports that Rich had done business with rogue states Iraq and Iran. As Rep. Lamar Smith, R-Texas, told the New York Times, 'If a Republican official had engaged in this kind of activity, he would never receive Senate confirmation.'"

There were other odd issues about this case, including that he recommended to a friend of Rich to hire a lawyer named Jack Quinn. Why would Holder put himself into a potential conflict of interest by doing this? Although Eric Holder has never explained himself, a House Committee report later revealed that Holder was seeking Quinn's support in order to be appointed Attorney General in a potential Al Gore administration. At best, this shows a lack of judgment that is generally not desired in a future Attorney General. Despite this record, Obama appointed him anyway.

The first controversy that would engulf the Department of Justice during Holder's tenure was the Black Panther case. This incident involved a video that showed two self-described Black Panther's, dressed in para-military garb, intimidating white voters at a Philadelphia polling station. Voter intimidation is illegal, and the case against the accused, backed up by videotape, was strong. Bartle Bull, a former civil rights lawyer and publisher of the left wing village voice, called this incident *"...the most blatant form of voter intimidation I've ever seen"*. At one point Mr. Bull heard one yell out *"You are about to be ruled by the black man, cracker!"*

Despite this, Eric Holder's Justice Department, with the defendants offering no legal defense, dropped the case.

One of the prosecuting lawyers, J. Christian Adams, resigned in protest over the handling of this incident. He also wrote a book ("Injustice: Exposing the Racial Agenda of the Obama Justice Department") that showed that this was not an isolated case. In Eric Holder's Justice Department, similar incidents were occurring all over the country, including outright corruption of the voting process. There is a reason why lady justice's eyes are covered with a blindfold. She must be impartial in all cases, or justice fails to have any meaning. What Adams' book appeared to reveal was that Holder's Justice Department was allowing the blindfold to be dropped a little in cases where race was involved (or at least in cases where the victims were white and the victimizers were black). Economist Thomas Sowell believes this book indicates that Eric Holder doesn't believe in a blind justice system. Rather, that:

"... Government's role in racial matters was not to be an impartial dispenser of equal justice for all, but to be a racial partisan and an organ of racial payback."

And that:

"A post-racial society is the last thing that Holder and Obama are pursuing."

This view is given further credence in light of Eric Holder's next major controversy, which is his consistent opposition to using photo ID in order to prevent voter fraud. Proving you are who you say you are doesn't seem to be that unreasonable when casting a vote. In fact, photo ID is used in a variety of instances in order to establish your identity. Cashing a check, boarding a plane, buying beer or entering a bar are but a few of the instances in which you may be required to produce photo ID. Having to produce photo ID for something as important as voting would just seem to be common sense.

Not only that, but there have been cases of large-scale voter fraud across the United States (including counties where the number of votes cast exceeded the number of people who could vote). This is why a bipartisan commission on Federal Election Reform in 2005 chaired by Jimmy Carter and James Baker, recommended that the use of photo ID be implemented.

Despite this, Eric Holder has fought this common sense measure every step of the way.

Incredibly, he has even compared this measure as an assault on voting rights equal to the civil rights struggles in the 60's. This is simply outrageous. Back then, African Americans feared for their lives if they showed up at a courthouse and attempted to try and register to vote. Comparing this to the requirement to produce the same ID that is required to buy booze is mind-boggling.

Eric Holder's poor judgment was also demonstrated by his attempt to prosecute 9/11 terrorist mastermind Khalid Sheik Mohammed in a civilian federal court as opposed to a military tribunal. This idea was so poorly thought out from the beginning it eventually had to be abandoned. Here are just a few of the problems in attempting to treat terrorists like conventional murder suspects that Holder apparently didn't consider:

- Terrorists are typically seized on foreign battlefields. Any evidence gathered at the scene are collected by soldiers in a war zone, not by forensics experts wearing white lab coats and gloves. Military tribunals, which are how enemy combatants are typically tried in, are set up to handle this. A civilian court is not.

- The best evidence gathered is likely classified, because making it public would compromise the sources and methods of US intelligence gathering. Military commissions are designed for this. They provide a secure environment in which classified evidence can be introduced without it being made public.

- Eric Holder was never able to articulate any kind of clear criteria as to why some terrorists would be charged in federal court and others would not.

- A civilian trial would have allowed the defendants to "lawyer up" and extend the trial for years. Justice delayed is justice denied.

- Holding such a trial in New York, with the media circus that would be sure to follow, would make the city an even more inviting target for terrorists than it already is.

Beyond these practical points is the larger issue of just how these trials would be viewed around the world. Holder, lacking all common sense, appeared to believe that civilian trials would be shining examples of the American justice system at work. But would they have been? When making his initial announcement Holder indicated that in his estimation (which, apparently, is never wrong), the case against the suspects was so strong that a guilty verdict was assured. First of all, it is extremely foolish to make such a statement. When you go to the judges, just like in boxing, you can never be quite sure of the outcome (see Simpson, O.J.). However, let's assume that Holder knows what he's talking about and a conviction is assured. What kind of a fair trial is it when the chief law enforcement officer of the land is all but saying that the outcome is pre-determined? Generally, it's in banana republics where the judge will announce, *"You will get a fair trial, and then we will execute you"*. How exactly does Eric Holder believe this puts the US Justice system in a good light? And what if KSM did get off, O.J. style? Would he just be allowed to walk?

Did either Obama or Holder think this through?

In the end, the attempt to try Khalid Sheik Mohammed in a civilian court was an example of both Obama and Holder's refusal to see 9/11 for it was, an act of war. Terrorists who engage in such acts are not members of American society who are refusing to obey the law. They are not shoplifters. They are enemies of the United States and are engaged in a war against it and everything it stands for. Only a far left partisan like Eric Holder could see it otherwise.

In my mind, however, the most outrageous decision made during Eric Holder's tenure was his decision to re-open the cases against the CIA agents for using "enhanced interrogation techniques". Essentially, these American heroes were tasked with the job of acquiring intelligence in order to protect American lives. The techniques they used had already been analyzed by Justice Department lawyers with no issues found. What's more career prosecutors from the eastern district of Virginia had already investigated the alleged abuses and found none that warranted prosecution. They also wrote extensive memo's describing why they had done so.

Eric Holder, over the objection of every living former CIA director including then incumbent director Leon Panetta, decided to proceed with re-opening the cases.

He couldn't even bother to read the memo's explaining why the cases had been closed (he admitted this later during testimony).

How would you feel if you were one of these CIA agents tasked with getting information from the scum of the Earth in order to protect your country, and later that same country decides to prosecute you for it? Would you think that made sense or was a just a award? What would happen if you were asked to perform the same task because a new high ranking terrorist had been captured, possibly with information on an upcoming 9/11-style attack? Would you be so willing to volunteer, knowing the way that Eric Holder had come after your peers? As you might imagine, the damage to the moral at the CIA was palatable.

To add insult to injury it was all a big waste of time. No one was ultimately prosecuted. Too bad Holder hadn't read the memos.

Suffice to say, Eric Holder has been an embarrassment as attorney general.

For bringing into question the impartiality of the Justice Department, for actively working against efforts to prevent voter fraud, and for his utter cluelessness in his attempt to have Khalid Sheik Mohammed tried in a civilian courtroom while undermining American security by attempting to prosecute law-abiding CIA agents, Obama should have asked Eric Holder to resign a long time ago. The fact that Eric Holder retains his position as attorney general is yet another reason why Barack Obama sucks.

Reason #23 That Obama Sucks - Gun Control

"I just want you to know that we are working on it. We have to go through a few processes, but under the radar" – Obama to Sarah Brady

Private ownership of firearms is one of the cornerstones of American liberty and American Exceptionalism. Befitting its status as the ultimate bottom up society, the primary protector of law and order in the United States is not the government, but the well-armed citizen. The world over, and even among it's closest Anglosphere siblings, top down governments have been working to unarm individual citizens, turning them into defenseless subjects needing government protection. Only the United States, with its glorious second amendment, stands in opposition to this trend. Currently, there are over 283 million privately owned firearms in the US. Half of all households own at least one gun. 73 percent believe the 2nd amendment reserves the right of a citizen to own a gun, whereas 70 percent oppose any law making handgun possession illegal.

It is in this environment that any politician must operate, and why it can be such a thorny issue for Democrats. Although most Americans are pro gun rights, a substantial part of the Democrats left wing base detests firearms and those who own them. In order to win office Democrats will often feel obligated to give a nod in the direction of the second amendment, while working through other means to limit them once in office.

Coming from the far left wing of American politics, this is exactly the template that Obama has followed. Whenever the political environment provides him with the opportunity, his true colors show. For example, in 1996 when running for the State Senate, Obama indicated that he supported a ban on handguns. As a state legislator he voted against a bill that would shield people who use handguns for self-defense in their own homes. When attempting to assure gun owners that he is not anti-gun, this is the answer he gave:

"What works in Chicago may not work in Cheyenne".

This is an odd position to take, as it indicates the he believes American's constitutional rights depends on where you live (not to mention that the gun control laws in Chicago are wildly ineffective). For these reasons and more, the National Rifle Association declared in 2008 that *Obama "...would be the most anti-gun president in American History".*

However, once in office Obama has had little opportunity to promote a gun control agenda. However, this lack of action doesn't mean he hasn't wanted to. As Sam Stein notes in the left wing Huffington Post:

"Faced with a Congress hostile to even slight restrictions of Second Amendment rights, the Obama administration is exploring potential

changes to gun laws that can be secured strictly through executive action"

This follows a pattern Obama has followed on ... pretty much everything. When his agenda is too radical for the checks and balances provided by the US constitution, Obama attempts to do an end run around it through executive orders. Why should gun control be any different?

So the question is, what is Obama's game with gun control? How can he get some kind of gun control enacted "under the radar"? What is the nature of his end run?

The answer appears to be through the cover of the United Nations via something called the Small Arms Trade Treaty. This international treaty is currently being negotiated in New York with the alleged aim of reining in unregulated weapons.

Like most ideas that emanate from the corrupt UN, this one smells bad.

First of all, the United Nations is the most top down, least accountable organization in the world today. If you wanted to imagine an organization that was the complete antitheses to America's founding, you would be hard pressed to find one better than the UN. In the view of UN bureaucrats, the legitimate use of force should be reserved for government entities only. This is diametrically opposed to the American idea of empowered citizens. In the United States, it is the individual, freedom-loving citizen who is the first line of defense. Government entities should support them, not the other way around. Most Americans know that the history of gun violence around the world is simple. It's the story of people with guns threatening and killing those who don't. Would the people in places like Sudan and Syria be better off if they had their gun rights protected? In situations like that the individual learns, usually too late, that the only people they can count on are themselves. You certainly can't count on the UN to do anything, even if you have George Clooney on your side.

The UN tries to make the defense that the treaty is only meant to enforce sales between nation states. This would make some sense, as 90% of all small arms trades are by governments such as the US, China, Russia, and Israel. However, the UN has refused to remove civilian firearms and ammunition from the scope of the treaty.

As former United States ambassador to the UN, John Bolton, put it:

"[The small arms treaty] is trying to act as though this is really just a treaty about international arms trade between nation states, but there is no doubt that the real agenda here is domestic firearms control."

Oh, and just to put a little more icing on this cake, guess who was elected to a top post at the UN Arms Treaty Conference?

Iran.

Can this thing stink anymore?

So, the UN wants to try and regulate the arms trade in small arms. How would such an enforcement body even work? What I would imagine they would do is to insist that countries that sign the treaty set up some kind of system to register guns. The bureaucracy that is set up to do this will accomplish two things:

1) It would create a permanent anti gun bureaucracy at the UN level which would work day and night to limit and undermine 2nd amendment rights
2) Once guns are registered by law abiding citizens it makes it that much easier to confiscate those same guns down the road. (Criminals of all stripes, including Iran, will of course just ignore this)

As Wayne Lapierre of the National Rifle Association puts it:

"If they get this through, then what comes along is the institutionalizing of the whole gun control-ban movement within the bureaucracy of UN – with a permanent funding mechanism that we [in America] will be mainly paying for,"

Prior to the election, Obama was not able to move on this treaty or any other significant gun control legislation. However, now that he no longer faces the threat of re-election, all bets are off. Ladd Everitt, spokesman for the

Coalition to Stop Gun Violence, has said that White House aides have assured him that the president intends to move on the issue in his second term. What form this will take is unknown. My bet is that it will be another unconstitutional end run in some form. We shall see.

In the end, most citizens in their gut know that Obama's support for gun rights is about as strong and heartfelt as his support for traditional marriage. He's just waiting for the right moment to "evolve". NRA spokesman Andrew Arulanandam puts it this way:

"We're not optimistic. We're planning for the worst. We've told people to plan for gun bans and a Supreme Court stacked with anti-gun judges. The president has a variety of options at his disposal -- we don't take any of them for granted."

His disingenuous and lukewarm support for the 2nd amendment is another reason that Obama sucks.

Reason #22 That Obama Sucks - Treating Britain Poorly

"There's nothing special about Britain. You're just the same as the other 190 countries in the world. You shouldn't expect special treatment." – an official in Obama's State Department

In actions both large and small, Barack Obama has rarely missed an opportunity to demean or downgrade America's "Special Relationship" with Great Britain. What is at the root of this disdain? As with most things, I suspect this disregard can be traced back to Obama's ivory tower mindset. Within the hallowed halls of academia, disdain for the idea of Anglo-American exceptionalism is strong. In their view, all cultures and countries are equal, and the idea of the nation state is passé. (This also explains Obama's strong support for supranational institutions like the UN and the European Union.) Others have put forward the theory that Obama's personal animosity to Great Britain stems from his grandfather's role as a Mau Mau supporter in 1950's Kenya. Although this episode, like so many stories in Obama's largely made up autobiography have turned out not to be true, it is none the less instructive and provides an insight into Obama's mental process. He wanted to align himself so strongly with left wing causes such as anti-colonialism that he made up part of his autobiography so that he could play the part. When this is considered, the reasons for his antipathy towards Britain become clearer.

Again, you have to judge Obama by his actions, not by his words, and his first actions when in office were telling. Within days of assuming the presidency he had a bust of Winston Churchill packed up and sent back to the British Embassy. Loaned as a gift from Britain, the Churchill bust was intended as a powerful display of solidarity in the aftermath of the 9/11 attacks. Viewed in isolation this incident can be written off merely as an example of Obama's amateurish public diplomacy on display. However, as time would tell, this sleight was merely the first of many to come.

The next humiliation that Obama had in store for Britain came when then British Prime Minister Gordon Brown made his first official visit to Washington. The reception Obama gave him was embarrassing. Not only was he denied a Rose Garden press conference, as is befitting a visiting dignitary of his stature, he was not even given a formal dinner. Brown's gifts to Obama were classy and thoughtful. They included an ornamental penholder made from the timbers of the Victorian anti-slave ship HMS Gannet, as well as a framed commission for HMS Resolute, whose oak was used to carve a desk that has been in the oval office since 1880. And how did Obama reciprocate? By giving Brown a set of 25 DVD's that can't be viewed on British DVD players. This was bad enough, but when the British press complained about Gordon Brown's poor treatment, a state department official responded:

"There's nothing special about Britain. You're just the same as the other 190 countries in the world. You shouldn't expect special treatment."

Very quickly, large organizations take on the characteristics and attitudes of their leaders. When Barack Obama can't even be bothered to mention the "Special Relationship" in any context, a message is sent. In this case, I believe the state department was accurately expressing the views of Obama and his administration. This view is further reinforced when no formal apology and no reprimand for the official involved were forthcoming. Apparently, these are only reserved for the French as well as enemies of the United States.

This disdain Obama has for Britain is humiliating enough at the diplomatic level. However, it gets to be a real problem when it rears its head in real policy.

An example of this is the Obama administration's betrayal of Britain in order to appease Moscow over a new START treaty. Britain's nuclear arsenal is small. As such it has an official policy of never confirming exactly how many nuclear missiles it has active at any one time. However, this is information that the Russians wanted. Washington lobbied London in 2009 for this information, but London refused. Nonetheless, the wikileaks cables revealed that Washington had *"secretly agreed to give the Russians sensitive information on Britain's nuclear deterrent to persuade them to sign a key treaty."*

Now, both START Treaties have disclosure and verification requirements, yet some secrets are and should be maintained. This is especially true in the case of a loyal ally that was not a party to the treaty and wishes to maintain a certain degree of confidentiality. None of this meant anything to the Obama administration. Although the new government of David Cameron quietly went along with the State Department's view once the details were released, what choice did it have? No matter how it is currently being treated, America is Britain's most important strategic relationship. It would do no good to publically admit that its most trusted friend had thrown it under the strategic bus in order to appease the Russians.

The next opportunity Obama had to demonstrate his disdain for the British came over his stated stance of neutrality over the ownership of the Falklands Islands. Here's the background:

The Falkland Islands have been a British overseas territory for longer than modern Argentina has existed. Once more the residents of the Falklands have never given the slightest indication that they have any desire, understandably, to join with the basket case of Argentina. If there is any question as to the sovereignty of the Falklands, it was settled during the Falklands war in which Britain bled blood and treasure to protect it. More than 255 British Soldiers died retaking the islands.

And what does Britain's greatest ally think about this?

Under Barack Obama, America is "neutral".

In fact, Obama goes out of his way to refer to the Falklands as "La Malvinas" (or the Maldives, a completely different set of islands, when he's not reading from a teleprompter), their Argentinian name. By doing so, he granted Buenos Aires President Cristina Kirchner a huge propaganda coup.

Currently, in an effort to divert the attention of the Argentinean people from her disastrous Peronist economic policies, Argentine President Cristina Kircher is taking every opportunity to sabre rattle and to lay claim to the Falklands. She is constantly working to get other Latin America countries onside to put pressure on Britain.

The European Union and even France strongly support the British position.

At this time it would be useful if Britain could count on its greatest ally.

But unfortunately, with Barack Obama as president, it can't.

Finally, when the chips are down there is perhaps no country in the world America can count on more than Britain. Currently, over 10,000 British troops are fighting alongside their American brothers in the Afghan Theater. This is a number greater than all of the other

European powers combined. Once more, the British actually fight and put themselves in harms way (currently over 400 British soldiers have died).

And Obama can barely be bothered to acknowledge this sacrifice in any speeches he gives.

This is in stark contrast to his predecessor, who frequently thanked the British armed forces and people for their contributions.

And who can forget this famous Obama quote?

"We don't have a stronger friend and stronger ally than Nicolas Sarkozy, and the French people."

Sorry, Mr. President. You do. You might want to say it once in awhile.

The reality of the world outside of academia is that all nations are not created the same. There are reasons why countries like Britain, the United States, and their sister countries in the Anglosphere are successful whereas others are not. Britain emerged to become a global power due to certain unique English ideals. Its greatest progeny, the United States, took those ideas even further than the mother country and became the global hyper power because of it. In history, culture, and outlook, a "Special Relationship" exists between the United States and Britain, whether Barack Obama knows it or not.

For constantly belittling and demeaning America's relationship with its greatest ally is another reason that Obama sucks.

Reason #21 The Obama Sucks - The Keystone Pipeline

"Blue-collar construction workers across the U.S. will not forget this [decision]."– Terry O'Sullivan, head of the Laborers' International Union of North America, on the Keystone decision

The proposed Keystone XL pipeline would have shipped between 500,000 to 700,000 barrels of oil a day from Canada's oil sands and North Dakota's Bakken Formation to the Gulf of Mexico. The pipeline, built privately by TransCanada, would have directly created 20,000 construction jobs and represented a 20 billion dollar investment in the American economy. The US Chamber of Commerce estimated that it would indirectly create 250,000 jobs over the lifetime of the project. Moreover, the President's own jobs council saw the need for more energy infrastructure projects, just like Keystone XL. In a report they stated:

"Continuing to deliver inexpensive and reliable energy is going to require the United States to optimize all of its natural resources and construct pathways (pipelines, transmission and distribution) to deliver electricity and fuel. The Council recognizes the important safety and environmental concerns surrounding these types of projects, but now more than ever, the jobs and economic and energy security benefits of these energy projects require us to tackle the issues head-on

*and to expeditiously, though cautiously, move
forward on projects that can support
hundreds of thousands of jobs."*

If there ever was a no-brainer decision, the
Keystone XL pipeline was it.

And what did Obama do?

He punted.

He delayed the decision on the pipeline until
AFTER the November election.

Why did he do this?

It can't be based on environmental or scientific
reasons, as the project had already been
studied to death. TransCanada had submitted
its application to the State Department (the
State Department handles decisions like this
that cross international borders) in September
of 2008. The project then underwent a 3-year
environmental review in which the risk to soil,
wetlands, water resources, vegetation, fish,
wildlife and endangered species were all
assessed. This scientific study concluded that
the environmental risks of building the
pipeline were minimal. Keystone also met 57
specific pipeline safety standards requirements
created by the State Department and the
Hazardous Materials Safety Administration
(PHMSA). The state of the art pipeline itself
would have been equipped with more than
16,000 sensors linked to a satellite that would
monitor the pressure of the pipeline 24/7.

Environmentalists tried to stoke unfounded fears that the pipeline would cross the Ogallala Aquifer, potentially threatening it with contamination in the event of an oil spill. This ignored the fact that thousands and thousands of miles of oil and natural-gas pipelines already travers the Ogallala, some for more than half a century, and none show risks of contamination. Even in the extremely unlikely event of a large spill, the State Department's impact study rated the potential for water contamination as minimal. This is because the soil composition mitigates or even out right prevents the downward migration of oil.

Another environmental argument is that the pipeline shouldn't be built as it will be transporting oil from the CO_2 producing oil sands. This argument falls flat on its face as the oil sands WILL be developed no matter what the US does. The only question is whether the oil will be shipped to the US or China. If it is shipped to China it has to be transported by tanker, which boosts the emissions of carbon dioxide and is much more environmentally dangerous. (Think Exon Valdez). Even Obama Energy Secretary Steven Chu, while not explicitly supporting the pipeline, did have to acknowledge that *"It's not perfect, but it's a trade off"* and that Canadian oil sands producers are *"making great strides in improving the environmental impact of the extraction of this oil"*.

Another point in the pipelines favor was that it was the definition of *"shovel ready"*. What's more, unlike the failed stimulus bill, private money would fund it. This is why 22 House Democrats sent a letter to Obama pleading that he approve Keystone. These included Senators Max Baucus (D–MT), Jon Tester (D–MT), Joe Manchin (D–WV), Ben Nelson (D–NE), Mark Begich (D–AK), and Mary Landrieu (D–LA).

And still Obama didn't approve the project. Why?

Once again with Obama, it all comes down to politics and placing his own short-term political considerations over the long-term needs of the country.

With an election looming, Obama realized he needed to throw a bone to his environmental base that were upset with him for his lack of action on cap and trade and climate change. However, in typical Obama fashion, he tried to have it both ways. He didn't reject the pipeline outright - he just delayed it. Unfortunately for Obama, to lead is to choose, and not leading when you're president has consequences. The irresponsible Keystone non-decision resulted is the United States surrendering its place at the front of the line to purchase Canadian oil. Oil is not difficult to sell, and Canada will be producing it with or without the USA. In contrast to Obama's dithering, China has been going around the world negotiating long-term deals to assure its access to energy. China understands the importance of energy for securing its economic future. Why doesn't Obama?

The ramifications for the business environment arising from this decision are even more disturbing. The Keystone decision tells investors that the U.S, as long as Obama is president, has an unpredictable business climate. Companies can invest years of effort and millions of dollars to seek permits and ultimately be stymied by politics.

Finally, Obama's decision has also put American security at risk. In the past Iran has threatened to blockade the 20 percent of the world's oil supply that flows through the Strait of Hormuz. A privately funded pipeline project that would help stabilize America's energy supply is clearly in the national interest. This is why two years ago; Obama's State Department approved a similar pipeline constructed by yet another Canadian firm -- the Alberta Clipper by Enbridge. At the time, the State Department said approval was granted because *"the department found that the addition of crude oil pipeline capacity between Canada and the United States would advance a number of strategic interests of the United States. These included increasing the diversity of available supplies among the United States' worldwide crude oil sources."*

With Obama's re-election the Keystone pipeline remains in limbo. There is some optimism that it will be approved, but with Obama who knows? Regardless, this politically minded delay has caused serious damage to the investment climate in the US and weakened American energy security. For putting his own short-term political interests ahead of the needs of the unemployed and America's energy security is another reason that Obama sucks.

Reason #20 That Obama Sucks - Reneging on the Missile Shield

"The Czech Republic and Poland have been courageous in agreeing to host a defense against these missiles. As long as the threat from Iran persists, we will go forward with a missile defense system that is cost-effective and proven." – Obama, speaking in Prague

During the Bush administration, both Poland and the Czech Republic signed agreements to host a missile defense system that the United States was developing. It was meant as a defensive measure against the threat of Iran acquiring long-range missiles to use with its presumed desire to posses nuclear weapons. Both the Poles and Czechs spent enormous political capital to convince their citizens to trust the United States and risk this deployment. Doing so, they hoped, would help solidify their relationship with America and give them some breathing space from their former masters in Moscow. This is why, in addition to the missile shield, Poland consistently backed the US in NATO and the UN, and even sent troops to Iraq. The Czech's also consistently supported their new American friends in international forums. They took these risks because they valued their freedom and, like so many countries, felt that an alliance with America was the best way to preserve it.

When rumors began to surface that America might renege on this signed agreement, it was met with skepticism. As Neil Gardiner put it, writing in *The Telegraph*:

"...if enacted, this would represent a huge turnaround in American strategic thinking on a global missile defense system, and a massive betrayal of two key US allies in eastern and central Europe. Such a move would significantly weaken America's ability to combat the growing threat posed by Iran's ballistic missile program, and would hand a major propaganda victory to the Russians."

Gardiner was exactly correct, which is why Obama was initially for honoring America's agreements and spoke in favor of the missile shield in Prague.

But 5 months later, shockingly, he changed his mind.

What happened?

Obama's defense secretary made a case that militarily; the missile shield did not make sense. The technology was not there and Iran remains a regional, not an intercontinental, threat. On this point commentator Ralph Peters agrees:

"I, for one, never believed this was the right system at the right place and time. The technology was immature, and Iran's a regional, not an intercontinental, problem."

Many commentators concurred with this assessment. From the purely military perspective of whether the missile shield was needed or would even work, there were real questions. The problem though, is that America had signed an agreement and given its word. There were larger geo-political considerations as well regarding what the missile shield represented. This is why Obama's decision, from a strategic point of view, was a disaster.

From its inception de facto Russian czar Vladimir Putin has opposed the missile shield, as he understood well what it represented. He has talked openly of what a tragedy it was when the USSR fell apart and lost its influence. His long-term goal is to rebuild Russia's military power while re-asserting Moscow's influence over its former client states. The American missile shield, whether it worked or not, was a direct challenge to this. This is why both the Poles and Czechs worked so hard to secure Washington's signature and why there was so much anger when the missile shield was cancelled. In fact, in the immediate aftermath, Polish Prime Minister Donald Tusk could not even bring himself to take a call from Washington explaining the decision (for which he apparently was not consulted). He had just been betrayed and thrown to the Russian bear. Who could blame him?

Obama's cancelling of the missile shield, and the way it was done, was a slap in the face to anyone who believed that a signed agreement with the United States was worth the paper it was written on. It showed Obama's weakening commitment to the transatlantic alliance and the defense of Europe. Worse, it demonstrated a willingness to sacrifice allies on the altar of political expediency while giving clear evidence that Washington could be intimidated by the Russian bear. If you were a leader of a former Soviet satellite like Ukraine or Georgia, how would you take this news? Would you still feel quite so secure that the US was serious about your desire to live in freedom?

Even noted Obama supporter Joe Klein was caught off guard by the move. Still believing, despite the utter lack of evidence, that Obama was brilliant; he wrote the following in *Time*:

"This is just speculation on my part. But I do hope that this anti-missile move has a Russian concession attached to it, perhaps not publicly (just as the U.S. agreement to remove its nuclear missiles from Turkey was not made public during the Cuban Missile Crisis). The Obama administration's diplomatic strategy is, I believe, wise and comprehensive – but it needs to show more than public concessions over time. A few diplomatic victories wouldn't hurt."

Were Klein's hopes correct? Did Obama actually have some brilliant diplomatic strategy that allowed him to extract some concessions from Russia? Did he perhaps have some commitments regarding Iran's nuclear program or maybe sovereignty guarantees for Georgia? How about getting some assistance in restricting arms sales to Venezuela? Insisting that Russia NOT sell S-300 anti-aircraft batteries to Iran would have been another good one. I mean, if you're going to throw allies under the bus, you should at least get something out of it, right?

The answer was ... no.

Barack Obama, the smartest president in history (in the world of presidential historian Michael Beschloss), got absolutely nothing for this betrayal.

When Obama cancelled the missile shield he was busily pursuing his "pushing the reset button" with Russia policy. He thought that by appeasing Russian aggression he would gain a more reliable partner in dealing with other issues. This view turned out to be exceedingly naive. For Putin, it was a demonstration of his forceful will overcoming Obama's weak, retreating United States. For America's allies, it was once again a demonstration of the great scholar Bernard Lewis's maxim that America was often

"...harmless as an enemy and treacherous as a friend"

For projecting American weakness and allowing erstwhile American allies to come further under Moscow's heel is another reason that Obama sucks.

Reason #19 That Obama Sucks-General Motors Auto Bailout

"I was betting on the American worker, and I was betting on American industry," – Obama, campaigning on what he regards as the success of the auto bailouts in Ohio

When Barack Obama assumed the presidency the American auto industry, in particular General Motors, was in real trouble. Hamstrung by high labor costs and benefits, not to mention cars that were just not selling, there was a real chance that both GM and Chrysler would have to seek bankruptcy protection. In order to prevent this from happening and in keeping with his belief in a top down, corporatist system, Obama made a massive bet of public resources into saving these firms. Today, both companies are doing better (GM just reported a record profit). Does this vindicate Obama's economic vision? Does it demonstrate that his top down style of economic management has some merit?

In a word, no.

In order to get a full appreciation of this decision, it is important to look at if from all angles. Not just the short-term and seen consequences, but also the long term and unseen. When viewed in this way, the negative long-term ramifications of Obama's decision on the auto bailouts become clearer.

Let's start from what would have happened if the Obama administration had done nothing. What would have occured? Most likely, GM (and probably Chrysler too) would have had to seek Chapter 11 bankruptcy protection. Does this mean that these companies would be finished?

Not at all.

The whole point of filing for Chapter 11 is to give potentially viable companies time to re-organize themselves. For example, back in the day before the advent of Chapter 11, let's say you were running a railroad company that was losing money. If you declared bankruptcy you might wind up having to tear up perfectly good railroad track for scrap in order to pay your debts. Chapter 11 came about because it recognizes that firms are worth more alive than dead. In the case of the railroad company, it makes sense to give it time to re-organize itself and bring in new management who might be able to run it at a profit.

Had the Obama administration not interfered in its heavy-handed way, this is what GM and Chrysler could have done. Filing for Chapter 11 would have given it protection from its creditors. New management is typically brought in who are committed to a successful restructuring. Under Chapter 11, brands, divisions, and facilities could have been sold off as needed. More importantly, GM could have reformed its labor contracts to bring them more in line with their competitors.

It is this last point that I believe the Obama administration did not want to happen. The UAW was one of Obama's biggest boosters. For an old school Chicago politician like Obama who believes in rewarding friends and punishing enemies, it was time for some payback on the public dime.

In order to understand fully what Obama did to accomplish this, I have to comment on the importance of respecting private contracts. One of the founding ideas that made America exceptional is that it was to be a land based on the rule of law as opposed to the arbitrary whims of kings. Simple, clear rules were to be applied equally to both the powerful and the weak. This is why the founders created the contract clause in Article V of the Constitution. It says that states are prohibited from interfering with the obligation to pay debts. It is meant to prevent governments from taking arbitrary actions on behalf of politically favored groups against those not so blessed.

In his bid to pay off his union friends, this is the clause that the Obama administration willfully ignored.

Here's how it's supposed to work. When you invest in a company, there are rules as to how you will be paid in the event that said company goes bankrupt. Secured creditors are given "absolute priority rule", which essentially puts them at the front of the line for any money that comes out of a restructuring. It is rules like this that make the US a much more inviting investment destination than, say, Bolivia. You

know in advance what will happen if the
investment goes south. Standing in line behind
them were the junior creditor claims, which
included the United Auto Workers Union.

What the Obama administration did was
essentially override these contracts. Through
political intimidation that would make Hugo
Chavez proud, they were able to browbeat the
secured creditors into only accepting 30 cents
on the dollar. The United Autoworkers, on the
other hand, received 50 cents.

In the short term the auto bondholders were
treated terribly by the Obama administration.
But what are the long-term consequences of
this action? If you are an investor, does this
action make you more likely to make a large
investment in Obama's corporate economy, or
less? If contracts you sign can be arbitrarily
overridden on the whim of the government,
and this is the precedent this action sets,
doesn't it make it less likely? In this case the
seen consequences are the jobs that have been
saved. The unseen consequences are all of the
thousands of new businesses that might not get
off the ground due to lack of investment.
Politically, trampling on the sanctity of private
contracts may have been good politics for
Obama, but in the long term it's bad for
America.

Another unseen consequence of Obama's top
down, corporatist actions is that companies are
often then guided by political goals, rather than
sound business judgments.

For example, one of Obama's big ideas is to increase fuel efficiency, and now that the government owns so much of GM it can really force these goals. But at what cost?

Here's what Obama's top down, know-it-all thinking doesn't allow him to understand.

Let's say you are comparing two cars to buy. The cars are essentially identical (look, price, etc.), except one gets much better fuel economy. You'd buy that car, wouldn't you? What's more, the car company would be more than happy to sell it to you. Why does anyone need Obama coming in like a car dictator into this equation?

What Obama doesn't understand is that there are always tradeoffs. When you increase the fuel efficiency, you have to give up something else. Perhaps you have to sacrifice safety to make a lighter car, maybe you have to change the appearance, and perhaps it just makes the car more expensive (hybrid and electric vehicles typically cost between $3000 and $20000 more). If you've read "I, Pencil" you know how complicated a pencil is; can you imagine a car? The arrogance Obama and his acolytes demonstrate by thinking you can dictate one change with no adverse consequences is simply astounding.

For GM's long-term viability, the fact is that the smaller, hybrid and electric cars don't bring in the profit margins that large cars and SUV type vehicles do. Those profit margins are needed to pay for the large UAW auto union contracts.

And how did the Chevy Volt do anyway?

The final point to make is another unseen, long-term consequence. When the government decides to invest 100 billion dollars in a company, that is 100 billion dollars that cannot go to other, more promising, firms. By attempting to preserve the old oak tree, it has snuffed out an unknown number of saplings from ever seeing the sun.

So, what were the final results of Obama's big bet with your money? Although he invested 100 billion dollars in various ways to bail out General Motors, the entire company, not just the percentage the government owns, is only worth 34 billion. In order for the taxpayers to break even on the investment Obama made for them, GM stock needs to be between $45 and $55 a share. Currently, it sits at $22. Obama claims his actions have saved a million jobs, but GM only employed 91,000 people in 2009. The entire US auto industry only employs 717,000. He managed to protect his friends in the unions, but he did so at the expense of weakening US contract law, which has likely had seriously negative effects on the economy. As well, by only tinkering with the UAW contracts, these companies will continue to be vulnerable in the future. And how does GM's future look? In the words of one analyst:

"The question for me about General Motors really is: Are they going to be able to sustain

this momentum over the long haul? If we are going to step back and say 'Was the bankruptcy a success or was it a failure?' it's really too early to say. We need to let a few more years pass to see if the new GM really is a new GM."

Ultimately, you just don't know. But by protecting GM this way Obama will now have to always protect it. If GM starts to go south, will Obama be able to let it go, or is he more likely to "double down" with the your money at the expense of non-politically connected companies and individuals? In order to pay off a political debt, this is the moral mess that the Obama administration created. The financial, political, and social echoes of this decision are likely to haunt America for as long as Obama is in office, if not longer.

Damaging the investment climate in the US while simultaneously wounding the economy with his top down corporatist philosophy is another reason that Barack Obama sucks.

Reason #18 That Obama Sucks-Failed Energy Policies

"We need to double-down on a clean energy industry that's never been more promising." - Obama, speaking about his energy policy

Strong economies, which are the source of the unmatched-in-history western lifestyle, are dependent on cheap and abundant energy. From the power that heats your home and turns on your lights, to the costs of transporting goods to market, to the energy it takes to operate a factory, it all needs energy. The cheaper the cost of the energy, the easier all of the above become. Like the blood that flows through the human body, cheap and abundant energy is what keeps a country strong and healthy. To try and restrict this energy flow makes about as much sense as intentionally blocking your arteries.

And yet, this is exactly what Obama has done.

Like all top-down ideologues, when Obama came into office he and his like-minded acolytes thought they had it all figured out. Fossil fuels that actually work were a relic of the past. Through wise government investment and management (under their direction, of course), they would build a new economy based on the faraway rainbows promised by green energy. Throughout the 2008 campaign Obama actually championed higher energy prices by imposing a cap and trade system. The idea would be to inflate the costs of fossil fuels (again, fuels that actually work) so that his subjects would start putting more thought into how to make energy sources like biomass and peat moss work. Or, as Obama put it:

"So if somebody wants to build a coal-powered plant, they can; it's just that it will bankrupt them because they're going to be charged a huge sum for all that greenhouse gas that's being emitted."

And of course what is a king without a royal court? Among his like-minded brothers would be eventual Energy Secretary Steven Chu, who openly mused *"Somehow we have to figure out how to boost the price of gasoline to the levels in Europe."* Like Obama, it never entered this Nobel Prize winners mind what these kinds of energy prices would mean for the typical American family. Driving to work, ferrying the kids to soccer practice or heating their homes all require energy. I guess none of these thoughts would enter the mind of an elitist who doesn't even own a car.

Then there is Interior Secretary Ken Salazar, who vowed to never open new federal offshore leases, even if gasoline reached $10 a gallon. *"We are setting the Department on a new path"*, is how he put it. Ken sounds like a reasonable, open-minded man, doesn't he?

It all must look so simple to make such plans for the little people while sipping on cognac in a university faculty lounge. However, reality and the dreams of central planners, no matter how clever, rarely coincide.

For the first three years of his administration Obama did nothing to increase United States domestic energy production. His focus was on his top down vision, which meant taxing and regulating proven energy sources to death while propping up pie in the sky politically correct energy schemes. None of it worked. For all of Obama's efforts, wind and solar generated less than 1 percent of American electricity in 2007. The Energy Information Administration estimates it might reach 13% of U.S. energy production if everything breaks right ... by 2035. Production from all renewable energy, including green unicorn favorites like biomass, wind, solar etc., increased just 12% between 2008 and 2011.

Turns out Obama, for all his alleged brilliance, knew as much about the energy industry as he does about job creation.

Meanwhile, while Obama was busy getting his education on how the real world works and the limits of his top down thinking, reality was busily changing America's energy future.

It turns out that America is energy rich. While Obama was throwing public money at his various schemes, new energy reserves were being discovered in Alaska and the Gulf of Mexico. It was also being found in such unexpected places as North Dakota, Pennsylvania, New York and Ohio. Thanks to new techniques like horizontal drilling and hydraulic fracking (which Obama had nothing to do with), the Institute for Energy Research estimates that there is enough natural gas in the United States to meet electricity demands for the next 575 years or heat homes for the next 857 years. There is more gas in the United States than in Russia, Iran, Qatar, Saudi Arabia and some place called Turkmenistan combined. As for oil, the U.S. Energy Information Administration estimates that the United States could soon overtake Saudi Arabia and Russia to become the world's top oil producer.

Isn't reality wonderful?

Of course, in order to exploit this embarrassment of riches, you have to have an administration that is committed to exploiting it. Unfortunately, Obama and his ideological soul mates in their various regulatory agencies have done everything they can to slow down production at every turn.

Under the guidance of the Department of the Interior's Ken Salazar, 77 leases have been revoked in Utah. Others have been suspended in Montana, delayed in Colorado, or out right cancelled off the Virginia coast. Offshore leasing revenue to the government has fallen from $9.48 billion dollars the year he took office to $36 million today. Permitting activity in the Gulf of Mexico is down over 60 percent from its historic averages while the Atlantic and Eastern Gulf of Mexico remains off-limits to energy exploration and production. Overall, leases on federal lands in the West are down 44 percent while permits and new well drilling are both down 39 percent since 2007. When this sad record is understood, it is clear why Swift Energy President Bruce Vincent is right to say that Obama has *"... done nothing but restrict access and delay permitting"*.

When faced with his disastrous record on domestic energy production and its all too predictable results, Obama, as always, attempts to spin and obfuscate his way out of any responsibility. One of his main distortions is to claim that domestic oil and gas production are up under his administration. While this is technically true, the reason it is up has nothing to do with his policies. He is claiming the benefits of permits and private industry efforts that started long before his term as president began. Everything he has done since has been to restrict and discourage domestic energy production.

His other main excuse is some variation of *" ... there are no short-term silver bullets when it comes to gas prices"*. Basically he is saying there is nothing he can do, that the most powerful man on the planet is powerless when it comes to oil prices. The fact of the matter is that a good portion of the price of oil is based on speculation. When speculators think production is going up, they'll speculate the price down (and vice versa). If Obama were simply to make some real, aggressive announcements that would boost domestic supplies, the price would drop. When President Bush lifted a moratorium in 2009, oil prices immediately fell $9 a barrel. In addition to this, a strong dollar not weakened by 1 trillion dollar plus deficits would also help. He may not want to admit it, but these are both under Obama's control.

Ultimately, Obama's blessed ivory tower vision of chasing green fantasies was utterly at odds with the reality of America's energy potential. When he wasn't wasting money on failed efforts like Solyndra he was killing real jobs by cancelling projects like the studied to death Keystone XL pipeline. While it is true that approved energy projects take anywhere from 10 to 15 years to develop, this is all the more reason to approve them NOW. In the meantime, the development of these projects creates real, high wage jobs for people like geologists, petroleum engineers etc. America's energy future is brighter than it has ever been. All that needs to be done is for the government to step out of the way and let it happen.

For weakening America through artificially high-energy prices based solely on his false renewable energy visions is another reason that Barack Obama sucks.

Reason #17 That Obama Sucks - Gutting Welfare Reform

"I was not a huge supporter of the federal plan that was signed in 1996" – then Illinois senator Barack Obama, commenting on the Clinton era 1996 welfare reform law

One of the greatest bi-partisan success stories that came from the Clinton era was welfare reform. Known as the Temporary Assistance for Needy Families (TANF) act, this law put in place real work requirements as a condition for receiving welfare. Although the left (including then senator Obama) hated the linking of welfare with a work requirement, the act itself proved to be a resounding success. However, it appears as though Obama has never bought into the logic of welfare reform, as with a stroke of his executive pen he has chosen to gut this signature piece of bi-partisan legislation. Here's what happened.

For decades, welfare was simply an entitlement. If you couldn't, or wouldn't, work, you simply received a welfare check, no questions asked. The concern with this approach was that this was creating a culture of dependency. Welfare caseloads were exploding while many able-bodied people remained on the dole. Rather than being a source of temporary assistance, welfare had become a hammock. People were wasting their lives staying in that hammock; as to get out of it meant having to give up benefits.

The TANF act of 1996 was the first attempt to tie temporary assistance to meaningful work requirements. It shifted responsibility to states with clearly defined boundaries as to what constituted work. From then on federal funding would hinge on states moving welfare recipients back into the workforce. The key thing here is that the legislation, passed with bipartisan support in congress, defined what would count as work. Left to their own devices, welfare bureaucrats have attempted to define work as attending Weight Watchers, taking hula dancing lessons and bed rest. The TANF act was written specifically to prevent these kinds of abuses.

The results of this act were dramatic. Brookings Institute scholar Ron Haskins noted that these reforms triggered an unprecedented decline in welfare caseloads, with the vast majority able to find work. 4.7 million Americans were moved from welfare dependency to self-sufficiency within 3 years of its enactment. The overall welfare caseload declined 54% between 1996 and 2004. Even more important, there is evidence that it improved the lives of those who were moved off welfare. Using data from the General Social Survey, Santa Clara University's John Ifcher showed that – despite the loss in leisure time and the stress in finding child care - single mothers were significantly happier about their lives eight years after reforms led them into the workforce.

The central insight from welfare reform is that people flourish when they earn their success, and this requires real work to do. Not only does work allow them to escape poverty, it allows them to lead more dignified and fulfilling lives.

Despite its obvious benefits, the left in America remains hostile to the idea of tying welfare to work. However, as polls show that 83 percent of Americans favor work requirements, they haven't been able to make changes to the act through legislation.

And this is where Barack Obama comes in.

Just as he has done with cap in trade carbon rules and elements of the DREAM (immigration) act, Obama has used an executive order to gut the work requirements of TANF. Essentially, Obama has done yet another end-run around congress and has claimed authority over every aspect of the TANF work provisions, rendering them meaningless. After the election, Health and Human Services can write any policy it chooses.

The Obama administration has attempted to push back on this by claiming that many governors, including Republican ones, have requested waivers so that they could have more flexibility. This claim is undercut by the fact that HHS will not accept any changes that might restrict access to aid – i.e. – reduce caseloads. On top of this, and more importantly, there is the question of how this was done. If there was a need for more flexibility in the legislation, Obama should have attempted to work WITH Congress and build a case for making changes to the legislation. The fact that Congress was not even consulted gives the game away, and is yet another example of Obama improperly using executive power to usurp the legislative branch.

There are currently over 70 welfare programs in operation today. The only one that requires people to look for work is TANF. If Obama were serious about creating programs that got people off government assistance, wouldn't it make more sense to look at expanding the ideas found in this program? How about food stamps, for example? The fact remains, however, that if you are only interested in expanding the number of people dependent on government, you would likely go after the one program that didn't do this. He can spin it any way he wants, but this is exactly what Obama has done.

For not consulting the Congress and unilaterally gutting one of the most successful bi-partisan legislative efforts in decades is another reason that Barack Obama sucks.

Reason #16 That Obama Sucks- Religious Freedom and the HHS Mandate

" ... secularists are wrong when they ask believers to leave their religion at the door before entering the public square" – Illinois state senator Barack Obama, speaking in 2006

On May 21, 2012, forty-three Catholic institutions, including the Archdiocese of New York and Notre Dame University, filed several lawsuits against the federal government. Their goal was to invalidate a Health and Human Services mandate requiring them to provide contraceptive and abortion services. Michael McConnell, an expert on the religion clauses of the First Amendment, called the move an *"unprecedented decision"*. The mandate, and Barack Obama's defense of it, demonstrates his lack of respect for the separation of church and state and his natural tendency for I-know-best, top down government.

"I hope these bishops are prepared to go to jail over this." - a friend of Daniel Henninger

Why are Catholics, as well as those individuals belonging to other faiths, so up in arms? To the Catholic Church, it is a core belief that artificial contraception and abortion are a violation of the natural order. To a Catholic, each and every marital act must of necessity retain its intrinsic relationship to the procreation of human life. Being forced to provide services that do exactly the opposite of that impinges on this belief.

The Obama administration, weakly, attempts to argue that churches are excused from the mandate. However, in bottom up America, churches are involved in the community in a multitude of ways. They run hospitals, soup kitchens, homeless shelters and immigration services. As writer Steve Chapman put it:

"A hospital may be named after a saint, founded by an order of nuns, replete with crucifixes and motivated by the teachings of Jesus, but too bad: It will be treated as the moral equivalent of Harrah's casinos or Bain Capital. Those in charge may regard birth control as inherently evil, but they will have to pay for it anyway."

As usual with top down decisions like this, unintended consequences abound. Employers that furnish health insurance have to follow the mandate. However, employers don't have to provide health insurance, and some with a religious mission may decide not to. When the District of Columbia passed a law that forced Catholic Charities to provide medical insurance to their same sex partners of its employees, the agency elected to simply drop coverage, for example.

"It's not about preventing women from buying anything themselves, but telling the church what it has to buy, and the potential for that to go further," - Sister Carol Keehan, president of the Catholic Health Association, representing some 600 hospitals.

86

Dropping insurance is not an option for larger employers, however. When you employ 50 people or more under Obamacare, you are required to provide health insurance or face a $2000 fine per employee. The bishop's anti-poverty agency, Catholic Charities, employees over 70, 000 people nationwide, which means they'd be looking at a fine of over $140,000,000 dollars. I suspect that a fine this large could put Catholic Charities in some difficulty. What's more, every dollar that goes to the fine is money that Catholic Charities CANNOT spend on their core service, which is helping the poor. Another Catholic institution in a similar boat is Notre Dame University, which could potentially face fines in the millions of dollars for similar reasons.

"The mandate vests too much unbridled discretion in the hands of government bureaucrats." – Hannah Smith, senior counsel for the Becket Fund for Religious Liberty

It is not just at the institutional level that the mandate infringes on religious freedom, it is at the individual level as well. Let's say you are a practicing Catholic with strong beliefs who works at one of these institutions. Due to the mandate, which you disagree with, your health insurance is dropped (So much for Obama's promise that if you like your health plan, you'll get to keep it). You are now forced to purchase your own health insurance on the new state-run health insurance exchanges. But here again, the Obama administration rejects freedom of conscience. The only policies available to you will include coverage for contraceptives and what the church considers "abortion drugs". No matter which way you turn, under Obama, the secular religion trumps your own.

"...The Obama administration was essentially saying 'to hell with you,' particularly to the Catholic community by dismissing our beliefs, our religious freedom and our freedom of conscience." – Pittsburgh Bishop Hannah Smith

And at its root, that is really the issue and why this mandate is so against American tradition and history. People escaping religious persecution founded America. In the past when individual states attempted to set up "official" religions, such as when Virginia attempted to establish the Church of England, the early colonists would not accept it. They exhibited the ornery independence of true citizens and would often plunge into the wilderness to set up new sects free of whatever the official government line was. This happened time and again, and is why the early attempts to establish "official" religions failed. This tradition eventually led to the establishment clause, which forbids the establishment of an official state religion.

This is why previous administrations have always treaded softly in this area by showing respect for American tradition, history, and the separation of church and state. For example, when the military relied on the draft, the Quakers were allowed to opt out due to their pacifism. When a Seventh-day Adventist was fired for refusing to work on the Sabbath, the Supreme Court said she was eligible for unemployment benefits. Prison officials have to respect and try to accommodate the religious practices of inmates.

With this mandate, Barack Obama and Kathleen Sebelius are going against this very American tradition. They believe that their secular religion of birth control trumps this history of religious freedom and diversity, not to mention the constitution. In direct opposition to what then state senator Barack Obama said back in 2006, the government is saying that Catholics can only believe what they want inside their churches. In the public square, they have to leave their religion at the door, no matter what the 2006 version of Barack Obama said.

" [I] cannot imagine a more direct and frontal attack on freedom of conscience" – Liberal Cardinal Roger Mahony

As of this writing, the mainstream press, which largely shares the president's secular outlook, have done their best to squash this story by simply not covering it. However, it remains the largest religious lawsuit ever launched in history.

For producing a mandate which violates the Constitution's Free Exercise Clause and is against the spirit of the Establishment Clause, as well as attempting to impose secular religious beliefs which put at risk all of the good work that non-governmental religious institutions perform, Barack Obama sucks.

Reason #15 That Obama Sucks- Solyndra and "Green Jobs"

"We can see the positive impacts right here at Solyndra. Less than a year ago, we were standing on what was an empty lot. But through the Recovery Act, this company received a loan to expand its operations. This new factory is the result of those loans...the true engine of economic growth will always be companies like Solyndra" – Obama, speaking at Fremont, California, May 26, 2010

"Obviously, we wish Solyndra hadn't gone bankrupt ..." - President Obama, March 21, 2012

Solyndra was a solar panel manufacturing company that received a large publically funded loan as part of Obama's "Green Jobs" program. Its story, right up until it went bankrupt, perfectly illustrates the limits of Obama's top down government-knows-best style. Although career politicians like Obama love companies like Solyndra, this kind of spending (which Obama calls 'investments") rarely ends well. The Solyndra episode demonstrates the limits of Obama's academic view of the world, as well as the fraud of his entire "Green Jobs" agenda.

Solyndra was founded in 2005 with the intention of manufacturing so called "Thin Film" solar panels. In theory, this kind of panel could be much more efficient than the traditional silicon variety. This technology was quite exotic and unproven. Commenting on past attempts to use thin film, Steve Hayward compared them to thin thigh diets. The promised benefits almost never matched what reality delivers.

Hope springs eternal, however, and in 2006 Solyndra executives approached the Department of Energy in an effort to secure a loan, which they intended to use to build a new manufacturing plant in Fremont, California. At the time, though, the government was much more interested in pushing nuclear power and finding ways to improve the electrical grid, so solar panels were not really on their radar. On top of that the final regulations for application approval were not finished until October of 2007, which meant that the review process spilled over into 2008. In an effort to expedite the process, the Department of Energy tried to force the Solyndra loan application through the Office of Management and Budget. OMB, however, found the application lacking and refused to approve it.

It looked like Solyndra was out of luck.

But then along came Obama, his stimulus program, and buckets of borrowed, public cash.

Otherwise known as the American Recovery and Reinvestment Act, the stimulus nearly doubled the amount of money the Department of Energy had to spend on clean energy projects. With Obama touting "green jobs" and "investing in tomorrow", Solyndra was in the right place at the right time. A 525 million dollar loan was approved on September 2, 2009.

And what happened?

Despite the loan, Solyndra filed for bankruptcy on Sept 6, 2010.

Its entire workforce of 1,100 employees was laid off.

The money loaned to it by the taxpayers will never be repaid.

How could the smartest president ever have been so wrong?

Once again, it comes down to knowledge and how decisions are made.

How do you decide whether investing in a solar panel company is a good idea? For a private investor spending his own money, he thinks about it long and hard. If he bets correctly, he makes money. If he's wrong, he loses it. It is this potential for losing your own capital that tends to focus the mind. The reason why companies like Solyndra need government-backed loans is because the market is indicating they are poor bets. Rather than investing in an iffy solar panel company, a private investor might find a better opportunity in a mop factory or some other business.

What are some reasons that the market might be indicating that solar panel factories might not be a wise investment? I can think of two big ones.

One reason would be because solar panels still have real weaknesses when it comes to generating power. Solar power depends on the sun. No sun, no power. Unless you're willing to run your hospital with no power you need to have a back up system, which is typically coal powered. It just isn't practical on a large scale. This has been the curse of solar power proponents for decades.

The second big issue is China. The top down government of China (which Obama admires for its ability to get things done) is spending a lot of money on manufacturing solar panels. What's more, China has access to cheap labor and raw materials. There are reasons why iPads and iPhones are manufactured in China. Why would it be any different for solar panels?

None of this matters to top down government knows best politicians, however. For a career politician like Obama, his primary goal is to get elected. Solar panels and "green jobs" are sexy and make for great photo ops. Mop factories, even though they may well be the more viable business, aren't.

When top down decisions like this are made, we all lose when they go bad. It isn't simply what one can see on paper that must be taken into account; but the unseen ramifications as welll. The $525 million lost on Solyndra is gone. The plant is closed and the people are unemployed. The unseen consequences, however, are just as important. For the money that Obama invested came from the private sector. It came from a private investor who could have invested in a viable mop factory, but now can't. By placing a bad bet based on political considerations, a truly viable business was strangled in its sleep.

This has been the experience of public spending on "Green Jobs" not just in America, but worldwide. Here are some examples:

- A123 Systems, which make advanced batteries, was given $279 million dollars. It lost $257 million last year, and is facing a shareholder lawsuit.
- First Solar, another solar power company, was given 3 billion dollars in taxpayer backed loan guarantees. They are now cutting jobs and their stock is at all time lows.
- Sunpower was given a billion dollars in loan guarantees. It lost half a billion dollars last year, and is now laying off workers.
- In Germany, Q-Cells, which was one of Germany's largest manufacturers, has filed for bankruptcy.
- Italy has announced it will cut renewable energy subsidies: "Industry Minister Corrado Passera says . . . that taxpayer subsidies doled out to the wind and solar power industries had generated "excessive" investments in the

sector... '*Italy has important goals to meet and even surpass,*' he said, but added, '*we need to do so without over-reliance on taxpayer resources.*'"

And so it goes. Top down politically motivated spending just make for poor investments. Beyond the purely bad economics of it, this kind of direct political spending also poisons and corrupts the political process. If you want to make money, how do you do it? In a bottom up economy you create goods or services that other people want. In a top down, Obama style economy, you use political influence and connections to gain power and wealth. In the case of Solyndra, one of the main investors was billionaire George Kaiser, who just happens to be a big Obama donor. Why risk your own money when your political connections allow you to risk the public's? As an editorial in the Chicago Tribune put it:

"He [Kaiser] discussed Solyndra with the White House as the company tried to get even more taxpayer backing and stave off collapse. Unable to secure a second government loan, Kaiser and fellow investors made a private loan — but they moved ahead of taxpayers in line for repayment when Solyndra defaulted. The administration said Kaiser never lobbied on behalf of the company. Emails contradict that claim."

It becomes a vicious circle of corruption known more widely as "crony capitalism". This is the top down economics as practiced in France. Public money is invested in companies, and in turn those companies make donations to the relevant political entities. Solyndra may have been the most famous example of this, but it's what occurs all over when governments favor one business over another. It's inevitable, and Obama's entire Green Jobs push has been a sterling example of this. As Eleanor Clift and Daniel Stone put it:

"Some of the biggest immediate beneficiaries of the green revolution, ironically, may have been politicians themselves. Executives of the top 50 recipients of the government's green-energy aid have donated more than $2 million to federal campaigns since Obama took office. Some of the biggest recipients of green stimulus money—including NRG Energy and Consolidated Edison—made six-figure donations to candidates and interest groups. The industry as a whole has ponied up more than $5 million from its executives and political action committees, a notable increase from a formerly quiet sector."

The only thing I disagree with from the above is that there is anything ironic about this. Rather, it is to be expected. When governments are giving away the public's money, the powerful will not only take advantage of it, but are sure to return the favor for future considerations. This is how crony capitalism in a top down economy works.

"...the true engine of economic growth will always be companies like Solyndra" says Obama. Sorry Mr. President, but you could not be more wrong. The true engine of economic

growth is the individual. It's the person who takes a risk to produce, or help to produce, a good or service that someone else is voluntarily willing to pay for. It's the little guy with the crazy idea, who no one has ever heard of, least of all self-serving politicians and their politically connected friends, that can change everything. It's not nearly as glamorous or exciting as a multi-million dollar solar panel factory, but it's what actually works. This is the real engine of economic growth, not companies like Solyndra. Obama just doesn't understand this.

For wasting public money on phantom green jobs like Solyndra while simultaneously weakening the economy and corrupting the political process is another reason that Barack Obama sucks.

Reason #14 That Obama Sucks - Undermining The Supreme Court

"Ultimately, I am confident that the Supreme Court will not take what would be an unprecedented, extraordinary step of overturning a law that was passed by a strong majority of a democratically elected Congress" – Obama, commenting on the possibility of the Supreme Court finding his health care law unconstitutional.

The American system of government is a delicate balancing act designed to ensure that political power never becomes too concentrated. This is why the founders wisely divided the federal government into the executive, legislative, and judicial branches. These branches were designed to be co-equal so that one would not easily be able to usurp the others. They also established a system of limited government with specific, enumerated powers in the constitution. However, as wisely as this system was set up, it is, in the end, only paper barriers. For this system to work well it requires individuals who respect and know how to operate within this system. An arrogant and ignorant man who does not do so can cause untold damage to this delicate balancing act.

Barack Obama is just such a man. His entire political career is that of a dilettante, assuming one office just long enough to float up to the next. He never took the time at any of his steps to the presidency to learn or appreciate how the American system works. As Laura Anderson, who served as a deputy chief of staff to the Republican leader of the Senate, noted on Obama's tenure in the Illinois State Legislator:

"He hardly showed up at all. He didn't even show up for picture day, and he didn't go to committee. He had no interest in the process, or in learning the process of being a good senator. He had no interest in government itself. He just wanted to stand on the Senate floor and give speeches."

When such a man gains the highest level of office in the land with essentially no experience at governing or getting things done WITHIN the American system, is it any surprise he'll do everything he can to go around it, through it, or over it as he sees fit? Is it any surprise that when he doesn't get his way he'll whine like a confused child? Like a bull in America's delicate china shop of checks and balances, this is exactly how Obama has behaved. And there is nowhere he has caused more damage than the disrespect he has shown to his co-equal branch of government, the Supreme Court.

Obama cavalier attitude with respect to the Supreme Court was first demonstrated with his unprecedented attack on it during a State of the Union speech. All but shaking his finger at the justices he condescendingly scolded them:

"Last week the Supreme Court reversed a century of law to open the floodgates for special interests, including foreign

corporations, to spend without limit in our elections"

Before we analyze the complete inaccuracy of the above statement it is important to consider the optics. The State of the Union is not supposed to be a partisan affair. It is meant to bring the entire nation together and chart a course forward. It is certainly never meant to be used as a platform to make a political attack on a co-equal branch of the national government. The Supreme Court, despite its crucial role in protecting a society ruled by laws rather than ambitious men, is nonetheless the weakest of the three branches. This is due to the fact that its members are appointed, as opposed to being elected by popular vote. Past presidents have typically recognized this, which is why, even when they have disagreed with individual court decisions, they have never stooped so low as to challenge the very legitimacy of the court. And make no mistake, Obama, like a gutless bully attacking someone who can't fight back, was doing exactly that. By attacking the court in this most public of forums, he was attempting to lower the legitimacy of the court in the eyes of the people. By doing so he was weakening the rule of law and one of the main pillars of the American system. As a former part time instructor (not a professor, as so many Obama boosters claim) of some aspects of constitutional law, Obama knew full well what he was doing. It was a shameful performance.

Aside from being rude, gutless, and unprecedented, Obama's statement was also a lie. As UCLA law professor Adam Winkler noted on the left wing Huffington Post, no less, *"...the court did not overturn a century of law"'*. Rather, *"...it upended a provision in the McCain-Feingold campaign finance law that was only seven years old. "*

Obama's next attack on the rule of law and its defenders in the Supreme Court was a little more subtle, but just as dangerous. When commenting on how he planned to pick a new Supreme Court justice, he noted that *"empathy"* would be among his main criteria. This line of thinking again betrays his lack of understanding of the American system. How can empathy ever be taken into consideration when deciding a court case? How would you feel if you had to go before a judge who has empathy for groups a, b and c, if you belonged to groups x,y,z? A judge is supposed to rule on the law, period. Questions of empathy and policy are to be debated in the political realm, not in the courts. If you were to take Obama's standard to its logical conclusion, you would in effect be repealing the 14th amendment, which guarantees "equal protection of the laws" for all Americans.

Obama's campaign against the court reached a new low when he commented on the then upcoming court case regarding the legitimacy of Obamacare. This is what the former part time instructor of constitutional law said:

Ultimately, I am confident that the Supreme Court will not take what would be an unprecedented, extraordinary step of overturning a law that was passed by a strong majority of a democratically elected Congress"

These comments are so ignorant and so obviously wrong that they are simply stunning. First of all, it is the job of the courts to overturn laws that are unconstitutional. That is what rule of law means. That is its job. If the Congress were to pass a law that denied women the vote, for example, the Supreme Court would overturn it as it violates the 19th amendment. It wouldn't matter if it were passed with a strong majority of a democratically elected Congress. In fact, the court typically overturns acts of congress every 16 months since the landmark Marbury vs. Madison case in 1803. There is nothing unprecedented about it, unless you believe the sun rising in the East and setting in the West is also "unprecedented". Again, this is the difference between the rule of law vs. the rule of ambitious men.

What is unprecedented is Obama attempting to put pressure on the court, challenging its legitimacy, before the court case is even decided. What's worse is that it appears to have worked. Chief Justice John Roberts at first seemed to side with those who would strike down the healthcare law and its individual mandate. However, many commentators believe that Justice Roberts changed his decision and allowed it by calling the mandate a tax. It appeared that Roberts, concerned about the courts reputation and standing, buckled under the not so veiled threats from

Obama. Time will tell if this was the correct action. That he felt he had to is a searing indictment of Obama.

For constantly working to undermine the legitimacy of the Supreme Court is another reason that Barack Obama sucks.

Reason #13 That Obama Sucks - The Iranian Green Revolution

"Obama, Obama, you are either with us or with them!" – pro-American demonstrators during the Iranian Green Revolution

Iran is not exactly known for its open and fair elections, but even by Iranian standards the presidential election held on June 12, 2009 took the cake. Despite a record turnout for the 4 candidates who were allowed to run (out of 476 who wanted to) the election was declared for the incumbent a mere 2 hours after polling stations closed. This obvious fraud was so brazen that it led to widespread outrage. Millions took to the streets in Iran and around the world to protest the results. However, the protests quickly morphed in something much more. They proved to be a spark that unleashed the desires of a people to bring down a tyrannical, misogynist, and corrupt theocracy. This became known as the Iranian Green Revolution, and with the proper support, it's possible the Iranian regime, an avowed enemy of the United States and the western world, could have fallen. One of the Iranian opposition leaders put it this way in a memo to the Obama White House:

"So now, at this pivotal point in time, it is up to the countries of the free world to make up their mind. Will they continue on the track of wishful thinking and push every decision to the future until it is too late, or will they reward the brave people of Iran and

simultaneously advance the Western interests and world peace."

This memo, along with the pro-American chants of the demonstrators, shows that Obama was given a historic chance. He could either support the demonstrators yearning for freedom, or the existing tyrannical regime.

It's too bad that he chose the regime.

Here's what Obama did during this unprecedented opportunity.

For nearly 3 days, Obama and his administration were utterly befuddled. Their only response was silence.

As pressure built and it became obvious that the protests were not going away, the Obama White House was forced to respond. Obama himself blandly noted *"some initial reaction from the Supreme Leader that indicates he understands the Iranian people have deep concerns about the election."* To this White House spokesman Robert Gibbs laughably urged *"vigorous debate "* between the protesters and the tyrannical regime that was having their heads beaten in. A week later, Obama did use stronger language, but he still tried to offer an olive branch to the mad mullahs. *"It's not too late"*, Obama said, for the regime to negotiate with the international community.

It was weak sauce, and without assistance from the USA, either covert or overt, the moment of danger for the Islamic regime receded into history. Today, Iran remains an implacable foe of the US as it expands its influence in the Middle East and rushes forward in an attempt to gain a nuclear bomb.

What could Obama have done, had he been so inclined?

First of all he could have offered up a robust condemnation of the Iranian regimes savagery free of his famous nuance. Past western leaders adopted the causes of Soviet dissidents like Natan Sharansky and Andrei Sakharov in an effort to bring down the Soviet Empire. Sharansky testified to the electric effect Ronald Reagan's Evil Empire speech had on lifting spirits in the Gulag. The news was spread cell to cell in code tapped on the walls. They knew they weren't alone, and that America was committed to their cause.

Revolutions such as the Green Revolution succeed when a transcendent moment is reached and the people, including those in power, realize that they've lost their mandate to govern. When beaten, arrested, and imprisoned, as many in the Green Revolution were, dissidents can easily succumb to feelings of despair and isolation. What Reagan understood is that when America speaks to the best aspirations of man, people listen. No matter what Obama really believes, America is not just another nation on the UN roll call list. To people who are truly dispirited, an American leader can give them a sense of, what's the word? Oh, yeah,

Hope.

Strong words, by themselves, from the American President, could have made all the difference. For once, Obama could have given a speech that actually mattered. Unfortunately, he was not intellectually equipped to recognize the moment and let it pass.

Beyond words, Obama could have helped the protesters by providing them with communication devices to circumvent the censorship of the government. In Reagan's day this was done with broadcast and copying equipment (as was done with the Solidarity movement in Poland.) Today it would have meant satellite phones and laptops for students.

If he really wanted to send a message, he could have threatened to cut off Iran's gasoline supplies.

What is even stranger is that the Obama administration, even putting the Green Revolution aside, has taken great pride in not providing any financial assistance to any political movement, party, or faction in Iran. In fact it has actively worked to suppress organizations that monitor this brutal regime. Among the actions it has taken:

- The Connecticut-based Iran Human Rights Documentation Center, a non-partisan group that documents Iran's human-rights abuses, had received 3 million dollars over the past 5 years for its important work. The Obama State Department cut their funding.

- Freedom House, another non-partisan watchdog group founded in 1941, also lost State Department funding. It supported efforts like Gozaar, a Farsi-English online journal of democracy and human rights, as well as other Iran related initiatives.
- The Obama State Department also cut funding to the International Republican Institute (IRI), which actively trained Iranian reformers and worked to connect them to like-minded activists in Europe and elsewhere.

What could possibly explain Obama's weak reaction to the Green Revolution, not to mention his government's subsequent actions? Why does he seem to be almost shielding the Iranian regime?

Once again, it comes down to the man.

Without any experience, Obama came into office possessed of the overwhelming self-confidence of a man who's never accomplished anything. As he told a number of liberal historians, he believed that simply through his powers of persuasion he could talk Iran out of its nuclear program. In order to do this, Obama needed the Iranian leadership to have legitimacy. The Green Revolution potentially undermined this.

In addition, Obama came into office determined to make a clean break with the policies of his predecessor. To Bush, Iran was a charter member of the "Axis of Evil" and its regime was illegitimate. To someone as educated as the sophisticated Obama, this was the formulization of a simple-minded cowboy. By showing deference and respect to the regime, (witness his use of terms such as "Supreme Leader" and constantly referring to Iran as the "Islamic Republic of Iran"), he was convinced he could make the Iranian regime see reason.

When the protests began to swell, this line of thinking utterly paralyzed Obama from taking any kind of action that might have helped. Reality was running smack up against his own leftist fantasy, and Obama proved he lacked the mental adroitness to accept this. Even when he managed to speak somewhat forcefully it was still couched in the language of splitting hairs and accommodation. As J. Scott Carpenter, a State Department official under George W. Bush put it:

"There has been a view within the Obama administration at a senior policy level that this Iran democracy program is a chit, and a chit that can be traded away to the Iranian regime"

Iran expert and human rights advocate Mariam Memarsadeghi thought that the Obama team saw the Iranian democratic movement only *"...as a wrench in the works of nuclear negotiations"*.

If the Green Revolution had been supported and succeeded, it would have been a game changer in the Middle East. For starters, it would have represented a decisive blow against Islamist radicalism in the same way that the collapse of the USSR was a mortal blow to communism. With Iran no longer acting as its standard bearer, Iraq and Lebanon would have found it much easier to grow their infant democracies. With their main financier and arms supplier gone, Syria would have been isolated, while terrorist organizations like Hezbollah and Hamas would have lost their patron. Most importantly of all, it offered the best chance for preventing Iran from becoming a dangerous nuclear power.

This is what was lost when Obama let the opportunity of the Iranian Green Revolution pass by. In an amazing display of arrogance and incompetence, he thought he could reason with people who have made it a policy of being unreasonable for more than 30 years. He bet everything on changing the current regimes nuclear policy, and didn't realize he had the opportunity to accomplish so much more by changing the regime itself.

For not supporting the Iranian Green Revolution and blowing a historic opportunity is another reason that Barack Obama sucks.

Reason #12 That Obama Sucks - Fast and Furious

"There have been problems ... I, uh, I had heard on the news about this story that uh... Fast and Furious, where – ah, allegedly, ah, guns were being run into Mexico and ATF knew about it but didn't, ah, apprehend those who had sent it." – Barack Obama, speaking on Fast and Furious

When the liberal media gets in the mood to pat itself on the back or reminisce about the "Good Old Days", nothing does it for them more than the famous Watergate scandal. In case you've forgotten, Watergate involved the break in of the Democratic National Committee headquarters at the Watergate office complex. When it was revealed that the burglars had cash on hand from the Committee for the Re-Election of the President (CREEP) and that President Nixon had attempted to cover up this fact, he (Nixon) was forced to resign. For the Obama Administration, Fast and Furious has the potential to be just as big and damaging. As far as scandal potential goes, Fast and Furious is just as big as Watergate, with the notable exception that over 300 people, including border patrol agent Brian Terry, were killed.

The liberal media have done their absolute best to bury this story. When they are forced to refer to it, it is often referred to as a botched gun running operation. They will point out that a similar program, known as "Wide Receiver", was run under President Bush.

Nothing could be further from the truth.

To understand why, let's first look at operation "Wide Receiver" and just what it entailed. Once we understand this, we'll have a better idea of why Fast and Furious is so bizarre.

The goal of Wide Receiver was to build a case against gun smugglers and drug cartels. The ATF wanted to find out who and where they were. It involved roughly 400 guns, all of which were equipped with RFID trackers. The Phoenix ATF and Department of Justice were involved, and the Mexican government was kept fully informed of the operation. Using "controlled delivery" protocols, radio devices, aircraft, and the RFID trackers were employed to track the guns as closely as possible. At least 1,400 arrests were made as a result of this operation. The program was shut down in October of 2007 when the smugglers discovered the tracking devices. That was the end of Wide Receiver.

Two years later, the Fast and Furious program began in October of 2009. The new Fast and Furious operation involved over 2000 guns, except that none of the "controlled delivery" techniques were used this time. No tracking devices were installed in the guns. There were no helicopters and no effort at on the ground surveillance. In fact, ATF agents have testified that they were ordered not to track the weapons and in cases where interdiction was possible they were ordered to stand down and watch the weapons walk.

ATF Special Agent John Dodson has testified how in one instance guns were sold to illegal buyers and then taken to a stash house. Acting against the orders of his superiors, Dodson kept the house under surveillance and when a vehicle showed up to transfer the weapons, he called in an interdiction team to move in, seize the weapons and arrest the traffickers. His superiors refused, and the guns disappeared without a trace. In addition to this Mexican authorities were not informed of the Fast and Furious operation.

None of this makes any sense. The only way this operation could have worked was if the intention of the program was to discover the weapons later at crime scenes where people were either injured or killed. Unfortunately and quite predictably, this is exactly what happened. Border Patrol Agent Brian Terry was killed by illegal immigrants using these weapons on December 14, 2010. In addition, Immigration Customs Enforcement Agent Jaime Zapata was also killed along with 300 Mexican peasants in separate incidents.

This is why anyone who refers to Fast and Furious as a *"botched gun running operation"* should be viewed with extreme suspicion.

It was not *"botched"*. It worked exactly as intended.

The question is why?

In order to get to the bottom of this, Congress has been holding hearings on the matter. During these proceedings Attorney General Eric Holder has done everything he can to mislead and slow down the process. For example, on February 4, 2011, Holder's justice department sent a letter to Senator Charles Grassley in which it was explicitly denied that the Obama administration had deliberately allowed firearms to be delivered to Mexican drug cartels. This letter contained the following statement:

"ATF makes every effort to interdict weapons that have been purchased illegally and prevent their transportation to Mexico"

This statement, which goes to the heart of the scandal, was false. On December 2, 2011 the department took the extraordinary step of having to withdraw this letter.

On June 14, Holder attempted to claim that his predecessor, Attorney General Michael Mukasey, was briefed about Wide Receiver. Here's what he said:

"If you want to talk about Fast and Furious, I'm the Attorney General that put an end to the misguided tactics that were used in Fast and Furious. An Attorney General who I suppose you would hold in higher regard was briefed on these kinds of tactics in an operation called Wide Receiver and did nothing to stop them – nothing. Three hundred guns, at least, walked in that instance."

Senator Grassley questioned the veracity of these claims and asked for evidence to back them up. Holder responded to Grassley's request by admitting that he had fabricated this smear against his predecessor. Here's the key section in a memo that Senator Grassley put out about Holder's stunning reversal:

"During a hearing last week, Attorney General Eric Holder claimed that his predecessor, then-Attorney General Michael Mukasey, had been briefed about gunwalking in Operation Wide Receiver. Now, the Department is retracting that statement and claiming Holder "inadvertently" made that claim to the Committee. The Department's letter failed to apologize to former Attorney General Mukasey for the false accusation."

How do you "inadvertently" lie? Lies are deliberate. You lie when you are trying to deceive someone. What is Holder hiding?

Holder has repeatedly claimed that no senior members in the Department of Justice knew about Fast and Furious. However, in an e-mail dated October 17, 2010 from DOJ officials Jason Weinstein to James Trusty, the following is stated:

"Do you think we should try to have Lanny participate in press when Fast and Furious and Laura's Tucson case are unsealed? It's a tricky case, given the number of guns that have walked but it's a significant set of prosecutions ..."

When presented with this evidence in black and white, Holder attempts to argue that "Fast and Furious" doesn't refer to "Fast and Furious". Amazing! Black is white and up is down in Eric Holder's world.

And this is where things get REALLY interesting.

As Eric Holder has repeatedly shown himself to be a dishonest witness the house committee has been trying to obtain Justice Department documents to get to the bottom of the issue. So far, fewer than 8,000 documents, a number of which would include duplicates, have been produced. Currently, the Oversight Committee is attempting to obtain an extremely small subset of the documents available. Specifically, those documents created after February 4, 2011 when the Justice Department falsely denied that it had allowed firearms to walk. In order to prevent these documents from shedding some light on the issue, the Obama administration has decided to assert a claim of executive privilege on the issue.

And just like that, Obama himself is now involved.

What exactly is executive privilege?

In order to preserve the separation of powers between the executive and legislative branches, it is well established that executive privilege can be used to keep communications directly involving the President confidential.

However Obama claims that he knew nothing of Fast and Furious and only learned about it *"on the news"*.

What Obama has done is to claim executive privilege on communications within executive agencies while asserting that neither himself nor his representatives were involved. By involving himself in this way he is on far shakier ground. As Senator Grassley put it:

"The assertion of executive privilege raises monumental questions. How can the President assert executive privilege if there was no White House involvement? How can the President exert executive privilege over documents he's supposedly never seen? Is something very big being hidden to go to this extreme? The contempt citation is an important procedural mechanism in our system of checks and balances. The questions from Congress go to determining what happened in a disastrous government program for accountability and so that it's never repeated again,"

What exactly is he hiding?

As of this writing, the following questions still need to be answered regarding Fast and Furious:

- Why did Eric Holder mislead Congress?
- Why did the Department of Justice lie to the Congress on Feb. 4, 2011, and what

was the process by which it reversed itself on June 14?

- Why was Fast and Furious implemented?
- Who came up with the idea?
- Why were ATF agents not allowed to track weapons?
- Why were Mexican authorities not notified?
- Why did Department of Justice officials approve wiretap applications when they apparently didn't read them thoroughly enough to know that gun running was involved?
- When did President Obama and Eric Holder learn of the operation?

As of this writing (December 8, 2012) Fast and Furious has seemingly been pushed off the pages by other news stories. This is not surprising as the vast majority of the Obama loving press showed precious little interest in this scandal to begin with. With Obama now safely re-elected it is doubtful that any more information that might reveal just what happened will be forthcoming. The ATF's Professional Review Board has recommended that four managers be fired over this incident, but this does nothing to answer any of the above questions, especially concerning Eric Holder's behavior throughout this episode. What's more it doesn't change the fact that the Fast and Furious scandal is another reason that Obama sucks.

Reason #11 That Obama Sucks - Gutting The Military

"...this is a budget in search of a strategy..." –
Max Boot, on Obama's "Strategic Reassessment" for the military

On June 15, 1953 the Queen of England and the Duke of Edinburgh boarded the frigate HMS Surprise in order to review the armada that had gathered to mark her coronation. Even at what turned out to be the twilight of the British Empire, it was an impressive site. Carriers with names such as Eagle, Indomitable, Illustrious, Theseus and Perseus lined the way, speaking to the power and influence that Britain still possessed. In all, some 300 ships, cruisers, destroyers, frigates and minesweepers took part in the review, and all were overflown by over 300 aircraft from the Fleet Air Arm.

Compare this impressive sight to what greeted the same Queen nearly 60 years later. Celebrating only the second diamond jubilee for a monarch in its history, the same Royal Navy could not even mount a cursory display. As one serving commander in the Royal Navy put it:

"It would have been just too embarrassing. There aren't many ships and those we do have are a long way away. It was just too difficult to mount a spectacle worth having."

What happened? How did the Royal Navy fall from "Britannia rules the waves" to a force not even up to putting on a show? As commentator Mark Steyn has noted, Britain's decline as a world power demonstrates the principle that you can have big government at home or an assertive national defense abroad, but not both. In a sense Britain, between 1953 and today, social and defense spending were basically inverted. The results are what you see today.

Which brings us to Barack Hussein Obama and the future of the American military.

On June 5, 2012, with no hearings and no input from Congress, Obama unilaterally changed a long-standing, bipartisan defense policy. This policy was predicated on maintaining U.S. strength capable to *"prevail against two capable nation-state aggressors"*. In Obama's Strategic Reassessment, the US would cut back to troop levels not seen since the end of the Clinton administration. In this strategy, the US would only have the strength to win against one aggressor, while delaying another. Obama tried to justify these cuts as part of a peace dividend. He had abandoned Iraq and the war in Afghanistan was winding down. Former General Carl E. Munday Jr. wasn't buying it. In his words:

"The new strategy is one derived not from risk analysis, but by fiscal constraints. One has only to ask, 'Would we have conceived this strategy had not we been driven financially to

do so?' I doubt anyone in the business of defense would answer 'yes.'
Our country is nearing financial desperation. Our elected leaders have been unable to deal with that threat. And the military establishment is being asked to pay a disproportionate portion of the bill to solve it. This is not without precedent. It has occurred of necessity at other times in our history. However, while the military culture is such as to respond to difficult orders with a 'can do' attitude and to conceive positive plans to deal with them, we should not deceive ourselves into believing that the new strategy is one of carefully assessed military choice rather than one driven by fiscal priorities elsewhere in our society."

Essentially, the military was paying the price for Obama's utter lack of leadership in dealing with entitlements and record spending levels. To do so would mean hard work and potentially offending his favored constituents. The left has typically never had much love for America's military, so as always, Obama chose the easiest path. For Obama, cutting the military is much easier than cutting NPR.

Obama's non-bi-partisan plan involves 500 billion dollars in spending cuts, which is on top of the 480 billion dollars he's already cut in his first 3 years in office. This will result in the weakest military posture since the days of Jimmy Carter, and the smallest forces since before World War Two. Although this affects the current size of the American military, and this is important, it is what these cuts do to the future military that is the most troubling. Without adequate funding, the military will be denied vital modernization equipment. The retrofitting of existing equipment, much of it badly degraded over the course of a decade at war, will be stretched or abandoned altogether. The new weapons systems that the US military counts on to maintain it's edge over more numerous foes will be weakened. Already such systems like the airborne laser and the Navy's hypersonic rail gun have been cancelled. What other vital weapons systems will be cut in the future?

What's more, Obama's vision for a dramatically reduced military is based on the assumption of a continued peace. If Obama appreciated history, he would know that assumption has been proven wrong again and again. As House Armed Services Committee Chairman Howard P. "Buck" McKeon put it:

"After every major conflict in the last century, the United States has cut its military, only to have to painstakingly rebuild it the next time our security is threatened. Sadly, this strategy repeats the mistakes of the past. ... History has taught us this is a perilous course, expensive in both lives and treasure."

Here is Obama's former Secretary of Defense on the same question:

"When it comes to predicting the nature and location of our next military engagements, since Vietnam, our record has been perfect. We have never once gotten it right, from the

Mayaguez to Grenada, Panama, Somalia, the Balkans, Haiti, Kuwait, Iraq, and more—we had no idea a year before any of these missions that we would be so engaged."

What Obama left wing ideology blinds him from seeing is that a strong military is not just about fighting and winning wars. It is about influence. A strong American military changes how foes and friends alike act. You need muscle to conduct a muscular foreign policy. Strength creates options, whereas weakness limits them. Or, as another president put it:

"History teaches that war begins when governments believe the price of aggression is cheap". - Ronald Reagan

One of the great responsibilities that America bears is to maintain a stable world order. America's prosperity depends upon open sea-lanes, an accessible Internet, and open use of satellites and space. Obama's reckless spending cuts weaken the sentries that make all this possible. No matter how he spins it, under his lack of leadership, America is growing weaker. As it always has, weakness invites aggression. It is only a matter of time.

For constantly working to undermine and weaken the American military is another reason that Obama sucks.

Reason #10 That Obama Sucks - Not Leading On Afghanistan

"I think he hated the idea from the beginning. He understood why we needed to try, to knock back the Taliban. But the military was 'all in,' as they say, and Obama wasn't." – an Obama advisor, on what he (Obama) truly thought of the surge he announced in Afghanistan

On the campaign trail Obama always referred to the war in Iraq as a war of "choice" and one that he would end as quickly as possible. Afghanistan, on the other hand, was a war of "necessity" that had to be fought and won. In campaign speech after campaign speech, Obama pilloried Bush for focusing on Iraq and thereby *"taking his eyes off the ball"* in Afghanistan. If elected president, he would devote the resources needed to win this necessary war. The question to ask now, as Obama begins his second term, is how Obama has managed this war of necessity since becoming commander-in-chief, and whether he was really serious about it from the beginning.

Giving a speech to the Veterans of Foreign Wars on Aug. 17, 2009, this is how he viewed the stakes in Afghanistan:

"This is not a war of choice. This is a war of necessity. Those who attacked America on 9-11 are plotting to do so again. If left unchecked, the Taliban insurgency will mean an even larger safe haven from which al-Qaida would

plot to kill more Americans. So this is not only a war worth fighting. This is fundamental to the defense of our people."

From this speech, Obama appears to be giving the impression that he considered the war in Afghanistan to be vital to American interests. However, as with all things Obama, talk is often one thing, action is another. Despite the importance his rhetoric appeared to put on the issue initially, there was little actually done. For example, in the first 3 weeks of September, he held but one meeting on this "war of necessity". Compare this to the five speeches he gave on five talk shows promoting his health care plans on September 20 alone. The General in charge of the Afghanistan mission at the time, Stanley McChrystal, had only met with Obama once since his appointment. Later though, Obama did find 25 minutes for him while he was on his way to Copenhagen in an effort to support the ultimately doomed 2016 Chicago Olympic bid. According to reports, McChrystal made the case for a "classic" counterinsurgency strategy. This would utilize a surge of 40,000 troops in order to secure the population and then later to win over the hearts and minds. In the words of Ralph Peters:

"...President Obama needs to make a decision: Either give the general the resources he believes he needs, or change the mission. "

But Obama did not make a decision. Months went by with no clear indication from the

White House as to what his Afghanistan plans might be.

Obama's indecisiveness took its toll on the allies who were also fighting and dying in Afghanistan. Then-British Defense Minister Bob Ainsworth pointed out that the lack of clear direction and purpose from Washington, along with the growing British death toll and the corruption of the Afghanistan Government, was making it harder to persuade the British public on the importance of the Afghan mission. This is how he put it:

"We have suffered a lot of losses. We have had a period of hiatus while McChrystal's plan and his requested uplift has been looked at in the detail to which it has been looked at over a period of some months, and we have had the Afghan elections, which have been far from perfect let us say.
All of those things have mitigated against our ability to show progress... put that on the other side of the scales when we are suffering the kind of losses that we are."

Time passed, until finally, some 3 months later, Obama was finally able to announce his hopefully well thought out Afghanistan policy. In a speech before an auditorium full of cadets at West Point he announced a surge of 30,000 troops (significantly below what his ground commanders had reportedly requested) to turn the tide against the Taliban. Incredibly, he also in the same speech announced that in 18 months those same troops would draw down. Why did he do this? From a military point of

127

view, it made no sense at all. If you were fighting with the Taliban you could only draw 2 conclusions from this:

1) Under Obama, the American will to fight was weak and getting weaker.
2) It should be possible to wait the Americans out. To the Taliban, the upcoming American election became just as important as it apparently was for Obama.

If announcing a withdrawal date didn't make sense militarily, why did he do it? Once again, for the campaigner in chief, it all comes down to politics. This is how the German magazine De Spiegel put it:

"For each troop movement, Obama had a number to match. US strength in Afghanistan will be tripled relative to the Bush years, a fact that is sure to impress hawks in America. But just 18 months later, just in time for Obama's re-election campaign, the horror of war is to end and the draw down will begin. The doves of peace will be let free."

Or, in other words, no matter what the consequences to the men and women under his command, Obama was throwing a bone to his rabid antiwar left wing base. By doing so, he weakened the chances of achieving victory, however ill defined it was. He was signaling, to friends and foes alike, "Don't worry, I'm going to end this war one way or another". Do you think making this announcement in any way helped the troops? By all appearances, and for only a re-election strategy, Obama proved that he was willing to undermine the efforts of America's military. Cynical is a word that could be used to describe such an action, but it somehow doesn't seem to be strong enough.

Despite being undermined by their commander-in-chief, America's military, as always, performed admirably. American forces were able to clear out insurgent strongholds in the heartland while at the same time helping the Afghan forces grow in numbers and professionalism. At this time 90 percent of operations now conducted are joint exercises between American and Afghani forces. In order to hold onto these hard won gains, senior administration officials realize that a significant American force needs to remain after the 2014 security turnover. These are needed in order to:

1. Conduct counterterrorism operations and ensure that Afghanistan never again becomes a terrorist sanctuary.
2. Convince the Taliban that American will is strong and cannot be outwaited. This is needed all the more given Obama's publically announced timelines.
3. Give the Afghan government more time to establish itself after the 2014 election.

Basically, all of the above could very well require an additional 2 years of heavy fighting beyond the 2014 election date. It's doable, but the American public is weary. What is needed more than anything is for the campaigner-in-chief to act like a commander-in-chief and robustly make the case for why these actions are needed. However, Obama just doesn't seem interested in doing the job. This is how Michael Gerson put it:

"At nearly every stage of Obama's Afghan War, he has surrounded even reasonable decisions with a fog of ambivalence. His initial Afghan policy review was a botched mess of vicious infighting, leaked classified material and mixed messages. His decision to pursue the Afghan surge seemed more of a reluctant concession than the expression of a firm conviction. His public statements on the war and its aims are rare -- mainly made in response to reporters' questions. Obama often pairs expressions of resolve with language of internal conflict and hesitance -- indicating a leader of at least two minds. And some people in his administration always seem willing to float an off-the-record trial balloon of accelerated retreat -- a circumstance Obama seems content to tolerate. "

In the end, you have to ask yourself how serious Obama was about the whole Afghanistan operation to begin with. From his subsequent actions as commander-in-chief, it would appear that his strong Afghanistan rhetoric was purely a political tactic designed to make him appear at least slightly hawkish on defense issues. It was classic Obama. By campaigning against Iraq as a poor "War of Choice" he was able to appeal to his hardcore anti-war base. By coming out rhetorically for Afghanistan as the "War of Necessity", he could simultaneously appear to be seen as strong on defense issues.

Of course, the verbal dichotomy that Obama set up was always a deception. All wars are ultimately "Wars of Choice". Even during Word War II, America didn't have to fight Nazi Germany or Imperial Japan. Such notables as Joseph P Kennedy and Charles Lindbergh argued that America could do well in a Nazi dominated world. World War II was fought, by choice, to rid the world of evil and help save America's friends and allies. When Obama evoked this false dichotomy, it was solely for the purpose of attacking George W. Bush. Now, however, when the moment demands one last push for his rhetorical "war of necessity", Obama remains silent. It is really quite striking. Despite making a lot of decisions his heart was never for, the men and women in America's armed forces have made it work. Now though, when it comes down to doing the one thing he likes to do, giving speeches, he chooses not to do it. Could it be that he knows that giving strong Afghanistan speeches might weaken his anti-war base during an election year? Can you think of any other reason?

It was said that Winston Churchill, a real wartime leader, *"mobilized the English language and sent it into battle"*. When the men and women of America's armed forces need their President to do the same, he's missing in action. America's brave military, and America itself, deserve better.

For not supporting the troops by forcefully making the case for victory in Afghanistan is another reason that Barack Obama sucks.

Reason #9 That Obama Sucks –
The Benghazi Scandal

"If four Americans get killed, it's not optimal"
– Barack Obama on the Jon Stewart show

On the anniversary of the September 11 terrorist attacks on New York City, the American consulate in Benghazi, Libya came under a coordinated terrorist attack. This attack resulted in the death of four Americans, including Ambassador Chris Stevens, diplomat Sean Smith, and former SEALs Tyrone Woods and Glen Doherty. Obama's reaction to this attack, as well as his attempt to deceive the American people as to its true nature, is another shining example of why he is unworthy of the office he holds.

On September 11 at 5pm Washington time, Obama, the secretary of defense, the national security advisor and the chairman of the Joint Chiefs of Staff were huddled in the Oval Office. At that time the consulate had been under a sustained assault for 90 minutes. At no time was military intervention considered as it was felt that to do so would violate Libyan sovereignty. Instead, the White House had the State Department request that the Libyan government provide assistance. None was forthcoming.

During the attack former SEALs Tyrone Woods and Glen Doherty were nearby in a CIA safe house. As soon as they heard the sound of gunfire they made repeated requests for military assets to be dispatched to the consulate. These requests were denied and there are unconfirmed reports that they were ordered to stand down. These American heroes ignored these orders and rushed to the scene. It is reported that they may have killed as many as 60 of the attackers before they themselves were killed by mortar fire. Both Ambassador Stevens and Sean Smith were killed, their bodies dragged through the streets like trophies.

In the immediate aftermath of the attack the Obama White House had a problem. For months one of its main talking points had been that Osama Bin Laden was dead and Al Qaeda was severely weakened. Having the first American Ambassador killed in 30 years was a strong demonstration that Obama's foreign policy was not as strong as he would have the American people believe. In order to distract the public from this successful terrorist attack the Obama White House scrambled to pin the blame on anybody but themselves. Despite knowing that it was false, the lie that was told to the American people was that the attack on the Libyan consulate was the result of an obscure YouTube video that no one had ever heard of. This deception included sending out UN Ambassador Susan Rice on September 16 to 5 Sunday talk shows to claim that, and I quote:

"We do not have information at present that leads us to conclude that this was premeditated or preplanned."

This was a boldface lie. CIA Chief David Petraeus has testified that he knew within a day that the attacks were performed by Libyan militia with ties to Al-Qaeda. Department of National Intelligence spokesman Shawn Turner told CBS News that:

"The intelligence community assessed from the very beginning that what happened in Benghazi was a terrorist attack."

This is the first scandal of the Benghazi tragedy. The Obama administration's attempt for a full week to cover up what really happened in Benghazi by pushing a story it knew was false.

The second scandal was that the Obama administration knew that the Libyan consulate was under threat prior to the attack and yet did nothing. On June 25 they received an embassy cable expressing concern over the rising Islamic extremism in Benghazi, noting that the black flag of al-Qaida had been spotted over several government buildings. Despite this, the Obama administration removed a well armed, 16 member security detail from Libya in August, replacing it with a couple of locals. Ambassador Stevens himself sent a cable on August 2 requesting additional bodyguards. This was in addition to several cables Stevens sent to the State Department expressing concerns about the security in Benghazi. Despite this, the Obama administration did nothing.

The third scandal is the administration's and Obama's response to the attack. It is now known that on the day of the attack a drone had been dispatched with a video camera to the Benghazi mission. This meant that the White House, the Pentagon, the State Department and the CIA were able to watch the attack via a live video feed. Despite knowing that an attack was underway, Obama apparently decided that diplomatic niceties out-weighed the safety of Americans in peril. After the election Ed Henry of Fox News asked the President if he gave any order to protect the lives of the Americans who were then under attack. Obama's less than adequate response was that he gave an order to do "whatever we could to protect our people in Libya". As of this writing we have no idea what "Whatever" means.

With few exceptions, the media have shown little interest in this story. Once again, it comes down to the fact that the mainstream media will do whatever it can to protect their guy. This includes during the election (witness CNN's Candy Crowley protecting Obama's false assertion in the second debate that he had told the American people that it was a terrorist attack the next day) and after. Below are some questions the media should be hounding Obama on, but are not:

1. Why was security in Benghazi weakened when it was known that al-Qaida was active in the area and despite Ambassador Steven's repeated please?
2. It is customary for American diplomatic institutions to be guarded by Marines.

Why were the Marines not guarding the consulate in Benghazi?

3. At what exact time did Obama became aware that the consulate was under attack? How did he react?

4. Was Obama able to watch the drone feed, which we now know was in the area?

5. Was the drone armed? If it was armed, why was it not used?

6. What exactly did Obama authorize to protect the consulate when it came under attack (whatever is not a reason)? What did Obama think would be done?

7. The entire incident took place over the course of 7 hours. Relief from American bases in Italy could have been had within 2. Why was the order not given?

8. Why were former SEALs Tyrone Woods and Glen Doherty requests for assistance turned down? Were they ordered to stand down themselves? If so, why?

9. Why did the administration attempt to blame the attack on a YouTube video, despite knowing within 24 hours that this was not the case?

One of Obama many deflections on this issue, which the media has allowed him to get away with, is that he would not speak through the media to the families of the fallen soldiers. Charles Woods, father of Tyrone, has stated that he would love to fly back to Washington, sit down with the President, and discuss what really happened in Benghazi. Obama, however, has not been willing to do this. In Mr. Wood's own words:

"The President, he's not willing to be transparent. It makes me wonder if he is trying to hide something. And what is it?"

With respect to Mr. Woods, I don't think Obama is trying to hide anything, as you can't hide what is in plain site. On his watch the Benghazi compound was left woefully undefended despite warnings that it was under threat. Once the attack was under way Obama failed in his role as commander-in-chief to marshal any of the resources at his disposal to protect those Americans in harms way. Once the tragic impact of his non-decisions became obvious, he had his administration attempt to obscure the issue by deliberating lying to the American people as to its nature, undoubtedly secure in the knowledge that a compliant press would cover for him. Sadly, he appears to have been right on that cynical calculation. Four Americans died, the president lied, and the press complied.

For not showing leadership when American lives were at stake and for later attempting to deceive the American people is another reason that Obama sucks.

Reason #8 That Obama Sucks - Undermining Israel

"You are absolutely wrong. For the past eight years Israel had a friend in the United States and it didn't make peace." – Obama, on why he took a tougher line towards Israel

Speaking to the Atlantic magazine and in other forums, President Obama has whined and expressed puzzlement as to why his commitment to Israel is constantly being questioned. Here again, the worst aspects of Obama are on display. Having never had to run for re-election with a record to defend, he can't seem to understand that past actions carry much more weight than any words he might say. No one questions John Boehner or Mitch McConnell's support for Israel because they actually do. Through his actions and words, Obama has demonstrated that his support is equivocal. Through a combination of his naivety, ignorance and overwhelming sense of his own abilities, he has put Israel in one of the weakest positions in its history.

To explain Obama's thinking process, you have to look at his past. Obama's intellectual background was nurtured in the radical left of American politics and the hallowed halls of academia. Both are notorious hotbeds of anti-Israeli sentiment. This is where he made alliances with such people as the infamous Israel bashing Columbia Professor Rashid Khalidi, not to mention sitting in the pews of the radically anti-sematic Jeremiah Wright for

20 years. I believe this is the reason why Obama had never, unlike his two predecessors, seemed to be in love with the idea of Israel. He may be able to recite some pro-Israeli tropes now and again, but he doesn't really believe them. What he does believe, like many of his left wing academic friends, is that resolving the Israeli – Palestinian conflict is the key to unlocking many of the Middle Easts ongoing problems, including achieving better relations with the Muslim world. What's more, the reason it hasn't been resolved is the fault of one party – Israel. Putting pressure on Israel would also allow him to distance himself from the extremely pro-Israeli views of George W. Bush. How could Obama behave in any other way?

His first example of applying pressure was his insistence that Israel halt settlement construction in so-called "occupied" territories as a pre-condition for peace talks. This was a certainly a new step as it had never been a precondition in 17 years of previous negotiations. What did he expect from the Palestinians? Nothing. No pressure was put on them at all.

Obama then went on his first oversees trip in July of 2009 and visited three Muslim countries – Turkey, Saudi Arabia, and Egypt. It was here that Obama made his famous Cairo speech, which he thought would signal *"...a new beginning between the United States and Muslims around the world"*. He did not visit Israel during this trip, nor has he EVER visited

Israel during his first term in office. People around the world notice things like this.

It was the contents of the Cairo speech, however, that were the most troubling. In it he seemed to accept the Arab narrative to explain Israel's existence, namely that Israel was solely created due to past Jewish suffering in Europe. Nowhere did Obama mention that the Jewish people have a more than 3000-year history in the Holy Land. What's more, only Israel merited special criticism from the president for their policy of settlement construction. On issues such as the abhorrent treatment of women in Saudi Arabia, to the Syrian backed assassinations of politicians in Lebanon, to the arrest and imprisonment of gay men in Egypt, Obama remained silent. The Cairo speech provided Obama with an opportunity to call on the Muslim world to acknowledge that Jews are as much a part of the Middle East and its history as are Persians, Arabs, Sunnis, Shia, Druz and Christians. He failed in that task. He didn't even try.

After his speech Obama called a meeting with Jewish leaders in July. As recounted in Edward Klein's book, "The Amateur", many of the attendees were shocked at how poorly Obama understood Israeli's position and expressed concern with his new tone as exhibited in the Cairo speech. Abe Foxman of the Anti Defamation League put it this way to the president:

"I agree with your goal to bring peace to the Middle East, but the perception is that you're

beating up only on Israel, and not on the Arabs. If you want Israel to take risks for peace, the best way is to make Israel feel that its staunch ally and friend America is behind it."

The famously thin skinned Obama, always shocked to hear other points of view, responded with this outburst:

"You are absolutely wrong. For the past eight years Israel had a friend in the United States and it didn't make peace."

This is Obama at his faculty-lounge worst and an example of what he and many of his advisors actually believe. To them, it is all Israel's fault, which is why many of them believe that Israel should be forced to make peace, even if it leaves it vulnerable to attack. In true top down, academic style, they believe that Israeli leaders who have lived their whole lives defending their country don't know as much as they do. Obama's response to Abe Foxman is an example of this.

The other major actions that have weakened the Israeli position against its intransigent enemies have been Obama's poor relationship, and at times shabby treatment, of Israeli Prime Minister Benjamin Netanyahu. As has been noted before, Obama is shocked when he hears views that are different than his own. Insecure and thin skinned, he tends to lash out when confronted with an individual who doesn't immediately see it his way or falls for his superficial charms. Unfortunately, the Israeli

Prime Minister can't afford to coddle an amateur. When leading a nation that is surrounded by enemies pledged to its destruction, he doesn't have the luxury.

Obama's poor, amateurish qualities were on full display in his treatment of Netanyahu after a March 10, 2010 incident in which a relatively low level official in the Israeli Interior Ministry issued a permit for 1,600 new housing units in East Jerusalem. The timing was poor as Obama had been continually insisting on settlement freezes (which Netanyahu had agreed to, for limited times, to no effect) and Vice President Joe Biden had just arrived that day. Netanyahu immediately apologized to Biden. Mahmoud Abbas, president of the Palestinian National Authority on the West Bank, used it as an excuse to call off future talks.

Obama was livid. Chicago politicians don't take perceived sleights lightly, and as he saw it, the Israeli's had purposely humiliated his vice president and sabotaged his peace plan. He had Hillary Clinton call Netanyahu and read him the riot act.

During a 43 minute harangue, Hillary give a series of ultimatums., each prefaced with the expression *"I have been instructed to tell you"*. These demands included:

- Releasing a substantial number of Palestinian prisoners (all of whom would have been guilty of attempted or successful terrorist attacks on Israeli citizens)

- Lifting its "siege" of Gaza (which Hamas was busily turning into an armed camp)
- Suspend all settlement construction in the West Bank and Jerusalem
- Accept that a symbolic number of Palestinians be given a "Right of Return" (something no Jewish leader can agree to, if Israeli is to remain a Jewish state)
- Agree to place the question of Jerusalem at the top of peace talks agenda

She finished off her harangue with this bluntly worded statement, which likely came directly from Obama:

"If you refuse these demands, the United States government will conclude that we no longer share the same interests"

For any Israeli Prime Minister, maintaining a strong relationship with the United States is of paramount importance. Netanyahu could do little but bite his tongue in the face of these outrageous demands. However, Obama was not quite done with him yet.

Ten days later, Netanyahu was invited to the White House where he was treated to further browbeating and humiliation. Netanyahu was afforded none of the pomp and circumstance that usually accompanies such a visit. Photographers were banned from the event, and, at one point, Obama left Netanyahu alone in order to have dinner with the following words:

"I'm going upstairs. Call me when you're ready to talk substance".

Humiliated by these grade school tactics, Netanyahu and his advisors were forced to cool their heels in the Roosevelt Room. At one point they were served non-kosher food, which some of them couldn't eat.

When Obama wants to make a show of his exquisite diplomatic sensitivity, he can. Burgers with Medvedev, bows to Abdullah, New Year's greetings to the mullahs, he knows how it's done. Likewise, when he wants to show his contempt, he knows how to do that too. To Obama, these sleights against Israel were meant to ingratiate himself to the Arab and wider Muslim world. As he said at the end of a speech to a group of Jewish congressmen and women:

"Our public disagreements with Israel gives us credibility with the Arab states and compels them to act".

So, in the end, was this view correct? Was the primary obstacle to Middle East Peace Israel? Were Obama's efforts at publicly putting pressure on America's stalwart ally in the Middle East worth it? Did publically humiliating Netanyahu bear any fruit? Did any new proposals come from the Arab side of the conflict?

Not surprisingly, the answer to all of these questions was no. Obama had completely misread the situation.

Why was he so wrong?

Veteran journalist Richard Z. Chesnoff, with more than 40 years of experience covering the Middle East, offered this assessment of Obama:

"In my opinion, Obama's problem in dealing with the Arab-Israeli conundrum doesn't come from the advice he's getting from his advisers, but rather from this one-man style and his inflated view of this own leadership talents. Obama believes that no matter what the odds against it, he can bring everyone together, kumbaya style, so that we can solve hitherto insoluble problems. Perhaps even more egregiously, he seems to have an exaggerated sense of his own depth of understanding of the Middle East, which is simply not borne out by his background or experience."

Adds Robert Lieber, professor of government at Georgetown University:

"The problem is naïveté in the Obama administration. The president came into office with the assumption that the Israel-Palestinian conflict is by far the most central urgent problem in the region – which it is not – and that it is the key that unlocks everything else in the region. And he and his advisors believed the [Israeli-Palestinian] situation

was ripe for progress, which it absolutely isn't."

It turns out that there is a reason why this conflict has resisted resolution for more than 60 years. When one side in a conflict is dedicated to wiping out the other at all costs, there can be no peace. For Obama and his cabal of Ivory Tower advisors, they apparently never ran this simply mental exercise.

What would happen if tomorrow, the Arabs put down their arms and stopped attacking Israel?

There would be peace.

What would happen if Israel unilaterally put down its weapons?

Israel would be annihilated.

That's the harsh reality.

The result of Obama's amateurish bungling and repeated sleights at America's only reliable Middle Eastern ally is that only 6 percent of Israeli's believe that Obama has Israel's best interests at heart. Understandably, this had led to a collapse in Jewish support and donations to his campaign. This may bother Obama and he may feel hard done by and misunderstood, but he has no one to blame but himself. He is going to have to look somewhere else for sympathy though as Israel is too busy trying to survive to worry about his feelings.

For weakening America's most stalwart ally in the Middle East through a toxic combination of his own ignorance and arrogance, Barack Obama sucks.

Update: - Obama's less than stalwart support of Israel has now born bitter fruit. For 8 days the terrorist organization Hamas, operating from its base in Gaza, subjected Israel to a steady stream of missile attacks. For Israel, surrounded by enemies on all sides, it cannot afford to be seen as weak or as losing, for weakness simply invites further aggression. Once the attacks began the only outcome that would be desirable for Israel would be a military victory of some kind. This likely would have meant a ground invasion that would give the Israeli Defense Forces an opportunity to route Hamas and destroy its stockpile of Iranian made missiles. The message has to be continually sent that attacking Israel in this manner will result in only one outcome, utter defeat for the attacker.

This did not happen, I suspect, because Obama did not give his support to Israel in private. Publicly the Hamas attacks forced Obama to support Israel. However, as with all things related to Obama, actions speak the loudest. Obama's actions (working with the corrupt United Nations and an Egyptian government which doesn't pretend to be anything other than Israeli's enemy) forced a cease-fire agreement on Israel before it could act, handing a significant propaganda victory to the Hamas terrorists and their Iranian and Islamist allies. Even the liberal Washington

Post had to admit *"...the commonly held view in both territories (the West Bank and Gaza) that the Islamist militants of Hamas – who refuse to recognize Israel – defeated their enemy, and they did it with weapons, not words"*.

In Gaza, billboards were erected that publicly thanked Iran for the missiles that granted them this great victory. Emboldened enough to speak in Gaza for the first time, Hamas leader Khaled Meshaal said the following before cheering crowds:

"Palestine is ours from the river to the sea and from the south to the north. There will be no concession on an inch of the land.
We will never recognize the legitimacy of the Israeli occupation and therefore there is no legitimacy for Israel, no matter how long it will take".

In his speech Meshaal made it clear that he wanted the Palestinians to claim every inch of the territory that make up modern-day Israel. As he did so the crowd chanted, *"Oh dear Meshaal, your army struck Tel Aviv"* and *"Oh Qassam, do it again, hit Haifa next time".*

Take note of that, *the next time*. All Obama's cease fire did was give Hamas time to re-arm for the next time while Iran now has an undefeated, confident ally on Israel's border.

Once again, Obama sucks.

Reason #7 That Obama Sucks - Losing Iraq

"...we'll be there a century, hopefully. If it works right." – Obama military advisor Gen. Merrill McPeak, on Iraq

Currently, the United States maintains, 40,000 troops in Japan, 28,000 in South Korea, and 54,000 in Germany. Why does it do this? There are two reasons. One is that Americans are a generous people, and are willing to assist others, even their former foes. The second reason is that the best American leaders are capable of great foresight. Helping to turn former enemies into stalwart allies and trading partners is in America's interest. Thanks to American power, Imperial Japan and Nazi Germany are thankfully relegated to the pages of history, while South Korea is a vibrant, prosperous country. It initially took a great deal of blood and treasure to win World War II and to protect South Korea. The subsequent American military presence ensured that those victories would not be in vain.

This idea is what Obama advisor General McPeak is referring to when he talks about staying in Iraq for a century. He is not talking about continuous fighting. He is talking about maintaining a significant presence so that the gains America made in Iraq were not lost. *"This is the way that great powers operate"* is the way he put it, when reflecting on America's long stay in Korea, Japan, and Europe.

When Barack Obama assumed the presidency on January 20, 2009, he was handed a war in Iraq that had been won. The troop surge he opposed had worked. The Anbar Awakening saw Sunnis fighting side-by-side American forces. The Shiite and Sadr militias had been taken down, and Al-Qaeda's forces had been decimated. U.S. casualties were at their lowest point of the war. All Obama had to do was to negotiate a new status-of-forces agreement (SOFA) to reinforce these gains, just as America had done before. By doing so, America would gain a reliable ally in this strategic region while simultaneously being able to offer up a competing model for what an Arab country could be.

And Obama blew it.

What happened?

Once again, Obama put his personal, short-term political considerations ahead of America's long-term interests.

Obama initially made a name for himself by aligning with the anti-war left when he famously said, *"I don't oppose all wars. What I am opposed to is a dumb war"*. At the time he was a young state senator from the ultra left district of Hyde Park in Chicago. This position did not take any great deal of courage to make. It was really the position you would have expected him to take, given his background and the district he represented. Once he took it, however, he became the darling of the anti-war left, and they held him up as their champion.

When he ran for the US senate in 2003, he continued to court and draw strength from the anti-war left by campaigning on "unequivocally" opposing President Bush on the war. Once he arrived in office, however, he voted for every war-funding bill, which annoyed his anti-war base. When he decided to run for president he needed this base again, so he changed in tune.

This was why when Bush finally approved of the troop surge; Obama used his famous good judgment to dig in, insisting that it wouldn't work, and that it would even make things worse. In the senate he forcefully advocated for a precipitous withdrawal of troops from Iraq by 2007. In 2008 he campaigned on bringing the troops home as quickly as possible.

Now, if you're an Iraqi leader, what would you make of all of this? You essentially have a choice. Do you align yourself with the Americans, or Iran? You know that Iran is not going anywhere and is constantly working to increase its influence in the region. On the other hand you have the United States, who is now led by a leader who has opposed the liberation of your country at every opportunity. What's more, in office, he has shown precious little interest in it. He rarely mentions your country in speeches and you have very little in communication with him. This same leader has also announced a new strategy in Afghanistan in which he has announced a withdrawal date for US troops in advance.

Would you trust this leader's resolve?

When the question of the extension of the status-of-forces agreement came up, US military leaders believed they needed a force of around 20,000 troops. This is the number needed to adequately train the Iraqis, help them build their US-equipped air force, be a player in mediating ethnic disputes, operate surveillance and special-ops bases, and establish close military to military relations.

If you were an Iraqi leader, what would you think when you learned that Obama had overridden his commanders, and wanted the troop levels to be between 3000 and 5000 troops?

A force so small that it would have difficulty protecting itself.

What would you think?

You would come to the only conclusion you reasonably could. Obama is not serious, and you cast your lot with the Iranians.

And this is exactly what happened.

When it became obvious that America under Obama was not serious about their country, Iraq was forced to adjust to the new realities. Since Dec 15, 2011, which saw the official end of the US military presence in Iraq, there has been a spike in violence, with more than 1500 people who have been killed. Prime Minister Nouri al-Maliki has been growing closer to America's sworn enemy, Iran, while the free press has come under increasing pressure. Even Kurdish leader Massoud Barzani, formally among America's staunchest allies, has seen it necessary to visit Tehran to seek accommodation with both President Mahmoud Ahmadinejad and Ayatollah Ali Khamenei.

Power abhors a vacuum. When the United States left, Iran was more than willing to step in. By abandoning Iraq, Obama has let it fall into the Iranian orbit. Instead of the hope of turning Iraq into a model for the rest of the Arab world we have yet another Iranian client state in its place. Obama didn't end the war in Iraq. What he ended was American influence in Iraq and the wider Middle East.

For shortsightedly surrendering the strategic territory that America had spent so much blood and treasure on is another reason that Barack Obama sucks.

Reason #6 That Obama Sucks - The Stimulus

"Shovel ready was not as shovel-ready as we expected" – Obama making a joke about his stimulus plan

When he took office with the American economy struggling, Obama needed a plan. Being a left wing ideologue, that meant that the government, in true top down style, had to do something. That something turned out to be his stimulus program. Other than Obamacare, the American Recovery and Reinvestment Act (the official name for the stimulus) was the biggest initiative of the Obama administration. In the words of vice-president Joe Biden, it was meant to *"literally drop kick us out of the recession".* The fact that it did not do this reveals the weakness in his thinking. Obama, and those who work for him, do not understand how jobs, or wealth, are created.

Keeping with what can charitably be described as his hands off style, Obama left the creation of his stimulus program to the Democratically controlled congress under Nancy Pelosi. With absolutely no Republican support (so much for bi-partisanship) the result of this was the largest economic recovery plan in history. At 820 billion dollars and over 680 pages long, it was larger than the Louisiana Purchase, the Manhattan Project, or the Marshall Plan. The stimulus was meant to have two phases.

Initially, the economy was supposed to be stimulated by a combination of middle class tax cuts as well as increases in food stamps and unemployment checks to get consumers spending. The tax cuts were in the form of tax credits, worth up to $400 a year for individuals and $800 a year for couples. These tax credits were spread over the entire year as to give people the impression that they had an increase in income, rather than a temporary bonus that they just might save. What this boiled down to is that the average person received an extra $10 a week on most checks.

The second part of the stimulus was meant to be invested in "Shovel ready projects" that would help pave the way for America's economic future. Roads, bridges, wind farms, solar panels, electric cars and high speed rail would all get sprinkled with a little bit of federal pixie dust from Washington. Obama's head of the Council of Economic Advisors, Christina Romer, felt that the stimulus was needed to keep unemployment below 8% and to get the economy growing again.

So what was the result of this top down spending (what Obama would call investments)? Amazingly, almost just the opposite of what was intended. Unemployment has never been BELOW 8% since the stimulus, and the recovery it has wrought has been the weakest since the Great Depression.

What went wrong?

To some left wing commenters like the New York Times' Paul Krugman, this largest government program ever was simply not large enough. Other, saner commentators, like Newsweek's Robert Samuelson, believed that the stimulus failed because it was always a political exercise and never a serious economic plan. In his words:

"It [the stimulus] was mostly a political exercise, designed to claim credit for any recovery, shower benefits on favored constituencies, and signal support for fashionable causes."

This is closer to the mark, as half the stimulus went in some way to democratically supporting unions, such as the SEIU, or unions at the federal, state, and municipal levels. Large amounts of money also went to silly projects, such as turtle tunnels, electric fish displays, and research on the effects of cocaine on monkeys. Nonetheless, and despite it's poor planning and execution, the stimulus did result in 41,000 miles of paved road, 600,000 low income homes were weatherized, and 3,000 rural schools were connected to the internet.

So why didn't it work?

The answer to this question gets to the heart of the lie of Obama top down, government is the driving force / knows best thinking.

How do you pull an economy out of a recession?

Jobs and real wealth need to be created.

However, no government program can create wealth. It can only take money from the private sector and spend it in the public sphere. It can only give with one hand by taking away with the other. And what's more, as government spending is usually done to meet political considerations, you are usually much worse off than before.

Real, wealth-creating jobs can only come into being when a person creates, or helps to create, a good or service that someone else is voluntarily willing to pay for. The prime mover in any economy is the individual citizen. This is what Obama doesn't get. True wealth creation ultimately has nothing to do with him. Everything he has done, including the stimulus, Obamacare, regulations and uncertainty about tax rates has made it less likely that individuals will take a chance and start a new business. It is individual citizens who build the businesses that build the economy. To paraphrase the president, Obama doesn't build that. To Obama, it's the government cart that pulls the private sector horse. In reality, it just doesn't work that way.

For wasting close to a trillion dollars while at the same time prolonging the recession is another reason that Barack Obama sucks.

Reason #5 That Obama Sucks - Obamacare

"I don't think we're going to be able to eliminate employer coverage immediately. There's going to be, potentially, some transition process: I can envision a decade out, or 15 years out, or 20 years out." - Obama, speaking at an SEIU Health Care Forum in 2007

The Affordable Care Act, otherwise known as Obamacare, is an example of the perfect storm of Obama's worst personal qualities combining to produce a terrible piece of legislation. Obama's inexperience, arrogance, and inflated sense of self-worth all played a part in its creation. Upon assuming office, his treasury secretary reportedly told him that his legacy would be to prevent a second Great Depression. For Obama, however, that wasn't enough. He would rescue the economy AND do healthcare. When a group of liberal historians suggested that Lyndon Johnson had difficulty managing a war and an ambitious domestic agenda, Obama grew testy. By the sheer force of his personality and brilliance, he could provide guns AND butter. What hobbled previous presidents would not stop him. After all, they were lesser men. They weren't Barack Hussein Obama.

What Obama, unmoored from any sense of reality, promised to do was to expand healthcare to between 30 and 50 million individuals without it costing more. How would this alchemy be accomplished? He really had no idea, which is why, just like with the stimulus program, he left the details to Nancy Pelosi's Congress. After an amazingly drawn out process a monstrosity of a bill (over 2000 pages) was produced. No one understood it, which is why Nancy Pelosi famously quipped:

"We have to pass the bill so that you can find out what is in it."

And that turns out to be one of the major problems with the Obamacare legislation. No one understands it, which is why the unintended consequences of it have been profound.

Take, for example, the tremendous negative impacts it has likely had on the already weak economic recovery. If you are running a business, it is incredibly important to understand your future costs. By itself, the Obamacare legislation has made this much more difficult and has likely put a real damper on new hires.

This is the problem that Mike Whalen, CEO of Heart of America Group (which runs hotels and restaurants) encountered when dealing with this legislation. As a CEO of a major company, he actually has on staff a number of experts he can turn to. When he asked them to summarize the future impact of Obamacare, one of them responded:

'We've gone to seminar after seminar, and, Mike, we can't tell you".

Brad Anderson, CEO of Best Buy, concurs with the assessment that Obamacare makes it impossible to achieve even a basic certainty about future personnel costs. It is bad enough for him, but he is even more concerned about its effects on new businesses before they even get off the ground. In his words:

"If I was trying to get you to fund a new business I had started and you asked me what my payroll was going to be three years from now per employee, if I went to the deepest specialist in the industry, he can't tell me what it's actually going to cost, let alone what I'm going to be responsible for."

This is how Obamacare already negatively affects major US companies. What about smaller firms, particularly those dealing with entry-level jobs?

Take the example of a businessman who owns 12 IHOP (International House Of Pancakes) franchises. In the restaurant business, many of his workers are part-time or change jobs every few months. As a result, he hasn't been insuring them, but Obamacare requires him to. If he doesn't, he has to pay a $2000 dollar penalty that he can't afford. This has forced him to cancel his expansion plans. Another interesting point is that Obamacare doesn't apply to employers with fewer than 50 workers. This provides a huge incentive for employers to stop expanding at 49 employees. If the owner of the 12 IHOPS had to deal with Obamacare from the beginning, it's likely he would have stopped expansion at 1 or 2 restaurants.

Are you beginning to get an idea of why new jobs are so hard to come by in the Obama economy?

Rapidly rising healthcare costs were another issue that Obama promised his reforms would address. The problem with rising health costs are that they crowd out other government programs and squeeze wages by diverting money into health insurance plans. However, despite his promises, Obamacare fails to do this. Even the governments own actuaries don't believe the cost control provisions in Obamacare will work. In 1980, healthcare costs accounted for 9 percent of GDP, including both public and private spending. In 2010 that figure rose to 17.9 percent. With Obamacare, that figure is expected to rise to 19.6 percent. Simply put, Obamacare does nothing to bend the cost curve of healthcare. As James Capretta of the Ethics and Public Policy Center put it:

"The president sold Obamacare by saying it would cover everyone, cut premiums, and solve the cost problem. No one believed him, of course, and for good reason. The law is a massive entitlement expansion, paid for with higher taxes and dubious Medicare cuts. There's no reason to think it will do anything except exacerbate our cost problems. The latest projections from the government – put together by economists and actuaries who essentially work for the president — confirm

that Obamacare adds to costs, not reduce them."

Another major failure of the act is that it adds to America's immense debt and deficit woes. When Obama campaigned for the act he repeatedly asserted that it would cost less than a trillion dollars and wouldn't bust the budget. This simply cannot be done. If you are going to add between 30 and 50 million Americans to a government program, that program is going to cost more. If Obama were honest, he would have admitted that up front and proposed a method to pay for it. Instead, he chose smoke and mirrors to create the illusion that Obamacare was meeting its goals. He did this by starting to collect the revenues for the Health Act, while delaying its implementation for 4 years. Basically, he was counting the revenues and hiding the spending so that over 10 years the costs would appear to be less than 1 trillion dollars.

Now that those near costless years of 2010 and 2011 have passed, the true cost of Obamacare is coming into focus. This is why the price tag associated with it has now jumped to 1.76 trillion dollars, almost twice Obama's original phony number. Even this assumption is likely under represented, as it assumes Medicare cuts that are unlikely to occur.

If all of the above were the only strikes against the health care act, it should be enough to end Obama's presidency. However, it is far worse than that. If you believe, as I do, that what made America great was that it reserved the maximum amount of sovereignty for individual citizens, Obamacare changes all of that. It "fundamentally transforms America" (in Obama's words) from the greatest bottom up society based on the idea of limited government into a top down, French style one. This is not what the founders envisioned.

One of the keys of bottom up style governments is the assumption that everyone is equal before the law. Whether you're a candlestick maker or the mayor, "No Parking" signs apply to everyone. Obamacare has introduced the idea of granting waivers that allow businesses, state and local governments, and unions to opt out of the health care law. So far, 1, 372 businesses have been granted a health care waiver by Secretary of Health and Human Services Kathleen Sebelius.

This raises the question that if the law is so great, why are these waivers being granted in the first place?

Beyond these concerns, what are the criteria by which a waiver is granted?
The HHS website pledges that the waiver process will be transparent. But it doesn't list what those criteria are or list those whose requests have been denied.

Union members are only 12 percent of the workforce; yet make up over half of the waivers granted. Is it just a coincidence that unions are among Obama's biggest supporters?

Just in April of last year, 38 waivers were granted to restaurants, nightclubs, spas, and hotels in Nancy Pelosi's congressional district. Pelosi's office denies she had anything to do with it, but does this pass the smell test?

America was built on the idea of equality before the law. By selectively granting waivers Obamacare is making a mockery of this. This kind of top-down crony capitalism thinking is a French way of doing things. It's certainly not American.

Worse than this selective granting of waivers is that Obamacare fundamentally changes the relationship between the citizen and the state. The primary way it does this is via the individual mandate. By stretching the commerce clause beyond recognition, it forces otherwise free citizens to purchase a product (healthcare insurance) simply because you're breathing. Defenders attempt to defend this over reach by comparing this necessity to that of buying car insurance. However, you can choose whether or not to drive a car. You can't choose whether you exist. This is NOT the American style of government. This is the French top down system, enacted on a scale never before seen.

"I don't think we're going to be able to eliminate employer coverage immediately. There's going to be, potentially, some transition process: I can envision a decade out, or 15 years out, or 20 years out." - Obama, speaking at an SEIU Health Care Forum in 2007

In an unscripted moment back in 2007, Obama pretty much outlined his plan for a complete government takeover of healthcare. The key is to move forward piecemeal. The government enacts solutions, which then creates more problems that the government then acts to solve. You are seeing this process in effect already. Instead of trying to understand the incredibly complicated Obamacare legislation, many employers are finding it easier to dump their healthcare plans (wasn't that one of Obama's promises as well? You'd get to keep your plan?) and pay the $2000 fine. This forces more individuals into the government plan and paves the way for a single payer system. What is the end result of this process? This is how Mike Whalen sees it:

"We've had an agreement in this country, kind of unwritten, for the last 50 years, that we would spend about 18 to 19 percent of GDP (gross domestic product) on the federal government. This is a tipping point. This takes us to 25 to 30 percent. And that money comes out of the private sector. That means fewer jobs. This is a game-changer."

He's right. Obamacare fulfills Obama's promise to *"...fundamentally transform America"* from a dynamic, bottom up society into a more European, top down social democracy. Like Europe, it will be the final step in transforming a nation of independent citizens into servile subjects. For attempting to fundamentally transform America via his unworkable health

care plan is yet another reason that Barack
Obama sucks.

Reason #4 That Obama Sucks - Exploding The Debt

"The problem is, is that the way Bush has done it over the last eight years is to take out a credit card from the Bank of China in the name of our children, driving up our national debt from $5 trillion for the first 42 presidents – #43 added $4 trillion by his lonesome, so that we now have over $9 trillion of debt that we are going to have to pay back — $30,000 for every man, woman and child. That's irresponsible. It's unpatriotic." – Barack Obama, July 3, 2008

Like the size of the universe, it is almost beyond human comprehension to wrap your head around the magnitude of the debt crisis facing America. Prior to Obama, numbers in the billions were casually tossed around. Post Obama, the word trillion is now commonplace. These numbers are so large they almost lose their meaning. Look at it this way. Imagine you earned $24,700 last year while you spent $37,900. For those of you who don't do math, this means you added $13,000 to your existing debt, which was already a mind numbing $153,500. How fiscally solvent does that sound? Now, replace yourself with the United States Government and add 8 zero's onto all of those figures. That is the size of the fiscal crisis that is looming for America.

Some economists believe that the US could default on its debt in 10 to 15 years unless some serious course correction is taken.

Congressman Mike Pence believes the 10-year figure is closer to reality, while Senator Tom Coburn believes it may only be 5 years away. If present trends continue, by 2020 it will take 19% of the entire world's GDP to finance America's debt. How long do you think the Chinese will be willing to work so that spendthrift America can live the highlife on borrowed money? By 2030 36% of all tax revenue will have to be used just to pay interest on the debt (it is currently about 11%). Don't worry though, the American taxpayer can cover this level of spending, so long as taxes go up, and not just on the "rich". This would mean raising the 10 percent bracket to 25 percent, the 25 percent bracket to 66 percent, and the 35 percent bracket to 92.

Doesn't sound like America to me.

All once powerful nations have fallen from grace due to the burden that government debt places on a countries economy. Throughout history it's always been the same song with only a few changes in the tune. England, France, Spain, Portugal, not to mention the Ottoman and Roman Empires. Decline always starts with the money, and the United States is not immune to these forces. The longer it takes for American leaders to adopt solutions, the more drastic those solutions will have to be. It could all happen quite unexpectedly. If the world stops buying US bonds, the crisis could hit quickly. America would be thrown into a depression, people's life savings would be worthless, taxes would explode, and the standard of living would plunge.

And what has Obama done in the face of this crisis?

In typical Obama fashion, he's made excuses while making the problem worse.

As candidate Obama noted in the opening quote, under that reckless rapscallion George W Bush, the debt rose $4.899 trillion during his two terms in office. President Obama, who only bears a superficial resemblance to candidate Obama, managed to beat that figure in only 3 years ($4.939 billion). The national debt stood at $10.626 trillion on Bush's last day in office. As of this writing the figure is now above 16 trillion, and it will be higher when you read this. What's more, the phony budgets that Obama has proposed, the ones that he can't get one Democrat to vote for, do nothing to address this issue. In his budgets the debt will hit 16.3 trillion by the end of 2012 and $20 trillion by 2016.

When forced to explain his sorry record Obama can only make pathetic excuses, typically blaming Bush. The fact of the matter is that even with the hated Bush tax cuts (which Obama kept in place when he could have raised them with a Democratic congress), federal revenue was at 18.5 percent of GDP. This roughly lines up with what the federal government has historically taken in going back to 1960. At this time the deficit was 1.2 percent of GDP and the debt was 36 percent of GDP. When the recession hit between 2008 and 2009 Bush did initiate a number of temporary anti-recession measures, such as his own stimulus plan and various bailouts. All of these measures Obama supported, and in fact he complained that the stimulus was too small. Would the situation Obama inherited have been any better if he had taken office a year earlier? The only difference would have been that Obama would have passed his gigantic stimulus that much sooner, which would have made the American fiscal situation that much worse.

Once again, it all comes down to the money. For most of recent history, the federal government spent about 20% of GDP on it's various functions. When the recession hit Bush ramped up a number of temporary measures (like his stimulus, the TARP program), which increased government spending. What Obama has done is taken that ball and run with it. In all of his proposed budgets (again, none of which were deemed serious enough to garner a single Democratic vote) he keeps government spending at these historic highs, and that's even before you include the ever-increasing costs of Obamacare. While he has been spending like a drunken sailor, his economic policies have led to the most anemic "recovery" in history. This has tanked the revenues that come into the government. In 2007, the federal government took in 2.57 trillion dollars. In 2012, it took in only 2.52 trillion. That's Obama-economics, and that's how you run 1 trillion plus dollar deficits for every year you are in office.

"People should learn that lesson about me, because next year, when I start presenting some very difficult choices to the country, I hope some of these folks who are hollering about deficits and debt step up, because I'm calling their bluff." - Obama, speaking at G20 summit, Jun 27, 2010

For most of 2011, when he wasn't busy making excuses, Obama promised that he would present a credible debt plan, as the above quote indicates. However, once again, Obama doesn't seem to understand that words do not equal deeds. Saving the United States from financial insolvency is going to take real leadership and courage, neither quality Obama has in abundance. As 2011 stretched into 2012 he talked less and less about his phantom debt plan until it fell off the radar scope altogether. In 2012 his Treasury Secretary, Timothy Geithner, was forced to confirm what everyone already knew. He conceded that although the Obama administration knew that the long-term debt was "unsustainable", the proposed Obama budget (again, not one Democratic vote!) would not deal with it. Under questioning from House Budget Committee chairman Paul Ryan, who has presented a plan that deals with the debt, Geithner commented:

"We're not coming before you to say we have a definitive solution to that long-term problem. What we do know is we don't like yours."

That statement is the Obama administration in a nutshell. Do not show any leadership yourself, and criticize those that do in the most

172

partisan way possible. Unfortunately for Obama, you don't get to pick your time in history. If you're the Prime Minister of Britain in 1939, your job is to fight World War 2, not reform the healthcare system. When Obama came into office America was involved in an economic crisis of which a major part was the growing debt. Rather than show any leadership on this issue he instead produced, in the words of the Wall Street Journal, *"...the worst record of any President in modern times"*.

For not showing any leadership on the issue that threatens the vey existence of America as a great nation is another reason that Barack Hussein Obama sucks.

Update: As of this writing (December 9, 2012) Washington is embroiled in discussions over the upcoming "Fiscal Cliff". If Republicans and Democrats cannot come to an agreement over said cliff, tax rates on everyone will go up and automatic spending cuts will be initiated that will be particularly harmful to national defense. With a weak economy and European levels of unemployment, this is not considered desirable by anyone. If Obama were any kind of a leader he would be involved in these negotiations everyday, working around the clock to hammer out a comprise. True to form, and not surprising to anyone paying attention for the previous 4 years, Obama is not leading. As he always does he is trying to float above it all by giving campaign speeches and playing golf. He's not paying a price for this despicable behavior as, once again, the press is covering for him. We've seen this before.

To understand Obama's intentions, as always, you have to look at his actions rather than his bland words. His actions reveal a man, obvious to everyone but the addlebrained media, who has no desire to cut spending or bring the deficit under control. Free from the threat of an election he can barely bring himself to talk about it anymore. This was demonstrated most clearly when his Treasury Secretary, noted tax cheat Timothy Geithner, presented the president's proposals to House Speaker John Boehner and Senate Minority Leader Mitch McConnell. It included a variety of tax increases and tax hikes, new spending plans and a permanent lifting of the debt ceiling. Talks about entitlement reform and spending cuts would happen later.

The proposal was so unserious that McConnell actually laughed out loud. It was the Wimpy (of "Popeye" fame)of budget proposals. I'll gladly pay for some spending cuts on Tuesday for increased spending and taxes today. Liberal columnist E.J. Dionne wrote that this should surprise no one, as this is the real Obama. He doesn't want to cut spending. Despite all evidence from his failed stimulus or the previous four years, he believes more government spending will help the economy. He doesn't want to cut; he wants to grow the government.

A friend of writer Alfred Regnery, who has watched Obama since his Chicago days, notes that two principles animate Obama. One is empowering labor unions; the other is that it is the government's job to redistribute wealth. Any proposal you see from Obama will have these two ideas lurking in the background. Obama's insistence on increasing tax rates on the richest 2% is a purely ideological play. If enacted they would lower the deficit from a projected 2012 deficit of 1.1 trillion dollars to 1.02 trillion. It's a rounding error. It won't solve anything. If the Republicans capitulate they will be broken. If they don't taxes will go up, which suits Obama just fine. Taxes will have to go up on everyone to pay for the size of government that he has no desire to reduce. It's just that this way he believes he can shift the blame. I'm not sure if he'll get away with it, but with the press in his corner, he just might. Regardless, Obama's behavior is that of a cynical Chicago Pol, not of the true leader that America desperately needs right now.

What can you say? Obama sucks.

Reason #3 That Obama Sucks - He's Not Bi-Partisan

"The pundits like to slice and dice our country into red states and blue states." – Barack Obama, speaking at the 2004 Democratic convention

After the vicious partisan divides that characterized the later Bush years, many Americans yearned for a leader who held out the promise of calming the waters and bring people together. In speech after speech, Obama presented himself as just that kind of figure. He promised to *"turn the page"* on the *"old politics"* of division and anger. He urged voters to choose *"...hope over fear, unity of purpose over conflict and discord"*. Most of all, he promised that *"I will listen to you, especially when we disagree"*. It was a compelling vision, and one that many Americans were eager to buy into. But was any of it real?

His past certainly provided few examples of a politician willing to take risks to cross party lines. In the real world that exists beyond soaring speeches, crafting bipartisan solutions is hard work. It involves taking risks, annoying your own supporters and making enemies. The real Barack Obama, the one that existed beyond the uncritical media halo, in fact made a career of avoiding these tough decisions. In the Illinois senate, for example, Obama earned a reputation for skipping tough votes. The examples of him working hard to restore a bipartisan political center simply don't exist.

This is a pattern that continued once he became a US Senator.

As a Senator, he wasn't part of the bipartisan "gang of 14" coalition that sought a way to end the logjam on judicial nominations. He initially joined a group led by John McCain to draft bipartisan legislation on ethics and lobbying reform. However, when Senate Democrats decided to write their own bill, Obama was only too happy to abandon the bipartisan option and vote with the Democrats. Incensed by the betrayal, McCain wrote the following in a letter to Obama:

"I would like to apologize to you for assuming that your private assurances to me regarding your desire to cooperate in our efforts to negotiate bipartisan lobbying reform legislation were sincere. I'm embarrassed to admit that after all these years in politics, I failed to interpret your previous assurances as typical rhetorical gloss routinely used in politics to make self-interested partisan posturing appear more noble."

The most famous example of Obama betraying his unifying, bipartisan rhetoric came during 2007 when McCain and Sen. Edward Kennedy were working together to craft a bipartisan bill on the always-contentious immigration issue. All who worked on the bill knew it would be tough, and they all agreed to offer no amendments. The reason being that if any one was adopted, others would be proposed, and the bill would quickly unravel. As Senator McCain noted, *"...we had to take tough votes, sometimes against the majority of our own party, in order to preserve the coalition."* One such amendment involved the sun setting of a guest-worker program, which the unions didn't like. Rather than hold firm and support the coalition, Obama broke ranks to support this amendment. The bill ultimately failed by one vote. Once again, when given the opportunity to be truly bipartisan, Obama didn't rise to the occasion. Senator Lindsey Graham, who was also a member of the group trying to push for immigration reform, put Obama's actions this way:

"He folded like a cheap suit. What it showed me is you are not an agent of change. Because to really change things in this place you have to get beat up now and then."

During his first year as a United States Senator, Obama racked up a voting record that was 82.5 percent liberal. This is hardly the record of a politician with a real desire to craft bi-partisan solutions. As one Democratic senator noted, Obama never became involved in any "transformative battles" where he might anger any of his parties interest groups. This same senator predicted that if Obama did become president " ... *If his voting record in the past is the real Barack Obama, then there isn't going to be any bipartisanship."*

How prophetic this turned out to be.

As president Obama has attempted to govern exactly as his past efforts would indicate, his post-partisan rhetoric revealing itself to be little more than empty words. As president he has never proposed innovative ideas that might cross ideological lines or build new coalitions. When presented with this fact Obama typically resorts to the blame game, blaming everybody but himself for this failure. The truth is that real leaders know how to work with the opposition to get things done. Clinton worked with Republicans to pass welfare reform and produce balanced budgets. Bush was able to work with Democrats to pass No Child Left Behind, the Patriot Act, and the Medicare drug benefit. Obama, on the other hand, strode into office and rammed through the most liberal measures on pure party line votes. From the massive stimulus program to a new healthcare entitlement to the largest deficits in American history, Obama proposed legislation that no Republican could possibly agree to.

Obama's hard left relentlessly partisan agenda turned out to be not so popular with the American people either, as the results of the mid-term elections demonstrated.

Faced with growing concern over the deficits and debt that he was running up, Obama proposed a bi-partisanship deficit reduction commission headed by Democrat Erskine Bowles and Republican Alan Simpson. The Simpson / Bowles commission was charged with presenting recommendations for entitlement reform in order to put the United States back on a solvent fiscal path. And what did Obama do when this bi-partisan commission that he appointed delivered its findings?

True to form, as it presented some tough public policy options, he ignored it.

The most egregious example of how much of a lie Obama's soothing bi-partisan posturing was came in his response to Paul Ryan's budget proposal. With Obama showing absolutely no leadership on the budget, Representative Ryan took it upon himself to craft his own proposal. It was a good faith effort that made serious attempts at tax and entitlement reform. In fact, it garnered so much interest that it forced Obama to respond to it.

Here's what Obama did.

He called a press conference, and invited Ryan to attend. He was even given a front row seat.

Obama then proceeded to attack this effort with a level of vitriol usually reserved for the waning days of a campaign. Here is an example of Obama at his "bi-partisan" best:

"This vision is less about reducing the deficit than it is about changing the basic social compact in America . . . There's nothing serious about a plan that claims to reduce the deficit by spending a trillion dollars on tax cuts for millionaires and billionaires. And I don't think there's anything courageous about asking for sacrifice from those who can least afford it and don't have any clout on Capitol Hill. That's not a vision of the America I know. The America I know is generous and compassionate."

This is the real Obama. He's not a post-partisan, reach across the aisle moderate. Rather, he's an old school Chicago style politician - nasty, unfair, dishonest, rude, and partisan to the core. If you were Paul Ryan, sitting there in the front row as the president attacked you and your plan while offering none of his own, could you ever trust him again? If you're going to work across party lines, you have to build a certain level of trust with the opposition. By attacking Ryan's plan in this way, Obama forever threw away the mantle of being a post partisan leader. Instead, he revealed himself to be an unserious partisan hack unworthy of the office he holds.

When you can't run on your record and have no ideas of your own, all you can do is attack your opponents in the most demagogic way possible. This is what Obama has done and continues to do. It is all the more galling in that as he engages in the rhetoric of a demagogue, he pretends he means the opposite of what he says. As he divides America, he pretends he is trying to bring it together. However, results speak for themselves. It is under his leadership that both the Tea Party and Occupy Wall Street movements were born. Gallop polling has revealed Obama as the most polarizing president ever to hold office since this kind of polling began. After four years of Obama, America is less united than ever.

In the end, the President has be President for all of America, not just the Democratic Party. At every step of the way, Obama has utterly failed in this task. Given how he's acted in the past, this isn't surprising. The media created image of Obama as post-partisan healer never matched the reality of the man or his record.

For practicing the politics of division at every opportunity while showing he has absolutely no idea how to bring the country together, Barack Obama sucks.

Reason #2 That Obama Sucks - He Is Economically Ignorant

"The private sector is doing fine. Where we're seeing weaknesses in our economy have to do with state and local government. "– Barack Obama speaking at a June press conference

When Barack Obama took the oath of office America was in the throes of the most brutal recession since the Great Depression. However, in electing Obama, the American people selected a man almost uniquely unqualified to deal with these challenges. Obama came into the presidency with no real business or private sector experience. As a community organizer and legislator, he learned how to divide up wealth for political gain, but never an appreciation for how it was created in the first place. It is his ignorance on this subject that has proven so damaging to his presidency and the country he leads.

"I think when you spread the wealth around; it's good for everybody." - Obama, speaking with "Joe the plumber" while on the campaign trail, 2008

With every statement, Obama demonstrates a faith in top down economic planning. He believes in the power of unaccountable bureaucrats to make wise investments that will somehow lead to economic growth. This is how Obama reportedly explained his economic philosophy in a dinner he had with a number of liberal historians early in his term:

"During his dinner with the historians, Obama indicated that he had a preference for a corporatist political system in which the economy would be collectively managed by big employers, big unions, and government officials through a formal mechanism at the state level. Also known as state capitalism, it is a system in which the government picks winners and promotes economic growth." – from "The Amateur"

There is nothing new about this corporatist system that Obama mentions. In fact, it's quite old. Its been tried before by fascist and democratic socialists in countries like Italy, Greece, Spain and Portugal. It never works. The reasons why this approach fails are two fold. First, any investments the government makes has to be taken out of the private sector in some way. The government has no money of its own and can only spend what it collects in taxes. The money that is uses to build a politically favored solar panel factory has to be taken from the not so politically connected shoe factory (or restaurant, or cleaning service, etc.) This makes it more difficult for the shoe factory to expand. Government can only give with one hand as it takes away with the other. The second reason is the fact that governments have proven themselves to be incredibly bad at making investment decisions. They may think that solar panels or high-speed rail are the waves of the future, but they don't know. Typically the only use these projects have is to get the politicians that sponsor them elected, rather than provide any kind of boost to the economy. Investments made by politicians are done for political reasons, not economic ones. History has shown that time and again, these kinds of direct government investments simply don't pan out.

"If some politicians had their way, there won't be any more public investments in solar energy. There won't be as many new jobs or new businesses. Some of these folks dismiss the promise of solar power and wind power and fuel-efficient cars. In fact, they made jokes about it. One member of Congress who shall remain unnamed called these jobs 'phony.' Called them 'phony jobs'. Think about that mindset, that attitude that says because something is new, it must not be real. If these guys were around when Columbus set sail, they'd be charter members of the Flat Earth Society." – Obama, speaking in Boulder City, Nevada, March 22, 2012

The question is, as always, who makes the decisions? Many Obama critics have often called him a socialist, and it is likely true that he would find very little to disagree with among the social democratic parties of Europe. However, as Thomas Sowell points out, his economic philosophy is probably better described as being fascist. Obama, with few exceptions, has rarely tried to own the means of production, as classic socialists would do. Rather, he prefers to leave businesses nominally in private hands while he seeks to control them through regulation. This allows him to offer politically desirable benefits while taking none of the blame for the adverse effects that may arise. For example, he can force insurance companies to keep adults on their parent's health plans till age 26. However, he is not seen as responsible when these same companies are forced to raise their premiums

"However many jobs might be generated by a Keystone pipeline, they're going to be a lot fewer than the jobs that are created by extending the payroll tax cut and extending unemployment insurance." – <u>Obama, Dec 9, 2011</u>

Whether you want to call Obama a fascist or a socialist, what is common in all of these left wing ideologies is that they have an absolute faith that some very wise people - always themselves and those like them - need to take the decision making power out of the hands of "ordinary" people so that they can be imposed by fiat. There is nothing wrong, in theory, with solar power or more fuel-efficient cars. But who decides? Who do you trust to make better investment decisions? You, investing your own money, or Barack Obama and his army of unaccountable bureaucrats?

"If you were successful, somebody along the line gave you some help. There was a great teacher somewhere in your life. Somebody helped to create this unbelievable American system that we have that allowed you to thrive. Somebody invested in roads and bridges. If you've got a business -- you didn't build that. Somebody else made that happen. The Internet didn't get invented on its own. Government research created the Internet so

that all the companies could make money off the Internet". – Obama, addressing supporters in Roanoke, July 15, 2012

Obama's "You didn't build that" speech was illuminating. For a brief moment, Obama took off his well-constructed moderate mask and revealed what he truly thinks. When you see the clip you can hear the passion in his voice. He truly believes that what makes a society work, the prime mover, is initiated by government. To Obama, it is always a government teacher (as opposed to the many other kinds of mentors you could have), or government built roads and bridges. It is seemingly the only way he can conceive of a society working. He doesn't understand and therefore utterly discounts the enormous efforts individuals take to get a business off the ground in order to pay the taxes that make those roads and teachers salaries possible. North Korea has perfectly fine roads as well, and yet the people just barely survive. Where are the businesses? It's something Obama has apparently never considered.

Despite his love for burning straw men, no one doubts the value of government roads and bridges, or even basic research. It's just that they are not the prime drivers of a wealth creating economy. His shockingly ignorant comments on the Internet demonstrate this. In Obama's world, the Internet was the result of government action and therefore justifies big government spending. Let's analyze this to see if Obama's claim holds up, or whether it's just so much water flowing under a government-constructed bridge.

Throughout the 1960's technologists of all stripes were working on different ways to connect separate communications networks. The federal government was involved in this effort, modestly, via the Pentagon's Advanced Research Projects Agency Network. However, this was not an Internet. Robert Taylor, who ran the ARPA program during the 1960's, has said this. *"The Arpanet was not an internet. An Internet is a connection between two or more computer networks".*

So, if the government didn't invent the Internet, who did? If you are looking for the prime mover in this case, you will want to look at Xerox PARC (Palo Alto Research Center). The same Robert Traylor who oversaw the Arpanet worked at PARC in the 70's. It was here that Ethernet was developed, which allowed computer networks to be linked together. They also developed the first personal computer (the Xerox Alto), laser printers, copiers, and the graphical user interface.

What prompted the invention of Ethernet was that its top researchers realized they couldn't wait for the government to connect different networks, so they had to do it themselves. *"We have a more immediate problem than they do. We have more networks than they do"* is how PARC's Robert Metcalfe put it. John Shock, who also worked at PARC, had this to say about their colleagues at the government run ARPA. They *"...were working under government funding and university contracts. They had contact administrators ... and all that slow, lugubrious behavior to contend with".*

The Internet was fully privatized in 1995, which also just happens to be the time it fully took off. Blogger Brian Carnell wrote this about the governments supposed role in creating the Internet in 1999:

"The Internet, in fact, reaffirms the basic free market critique of large government. Here for 30 years the government had an immensely useful protocol for transferring information, TCP/IP, but it languished. . . . In less than a decade, private concerns have taken that protocol and created one of the most important technological revolutions of the millennia."

The Internet you use today is only loosely connected to the government in anyway. Rather, it is the result of private companies working hard to innovate and create products and services that people will find useful. Companies like Google, Apple, Microsoft, Oracle, and thousands of others were not created because a government bureaucrat wrote a regulation or built a road. They were created through the dynamic efforts of individuals working together, and they deserve to be praised rather than sneered at.

Obama simply gives no indication that he understands this. It is the private sector that generates the wealth that makes the public sector possible, not the reverse. A private company can potentially build a road, a government without tax revenue from the private economy cannot. This is how Indiana Governor Mitch Daniels puts it:

"He doesn't understand where wealth and jobs come from. It comes from a successful private sector or not at all.
You know, we've got the biggest government and the weakest recovery on record. I think honestly, the president — this week he said, if I read correctly and to my amazement, he said the private sector is doing just fine. It's government that needs more money.
Well, government doesn't create wealth or income. It just shuffles it around and charges a price and cost for that service or disservice. . . .
Now, this is [a] tired and discredited theory. But I do think that the president sincerely believes it. And there, I guess, [is] a fundamental disagreement that the American people will have to settle this fall."

What have been the results of Obama's top down, corporatist philosophy? Try the longest period of sustained unemployment and the weakest recovery since the Great Depression. As a point of comparison during the Reagan recovery, more than 8 million new jobs were created. In September 1983 alone more than 1.1 million jobs were produced. Nothing Obama has done can compare to this, and as of this writing unemployment is going up, not down. Thanks to his policies, the Obama recovery is a largely jobless enterprise with people fleeing the labor force. After four years of Obama, Americans are poorer, less sure of their future, and frightened.

The conclusion is inescapable. Obama is profoundly economically ignorant and simply doesn't know what he's doing.

For giving no indication he understands how wealth is created in an economy while simultaneously imposing policies that have led to the weakest recovery during the modern era is another reason that Barack Obama sucks.

Reason #1 That Obama Sucks - He's Not A Leader

"The American people have come to realize that, in Barack Obama, they have elected a man as president who does not know how to lead. He lacks an executive sense. He doesn't know how to run things. He's not a manager. He hasn't been able to bring together the best and brightest talents. Not to put too fine a point on it, he's in over his head." – a liberal historian, as quoted in Ed Klein's book "The Amateur"

What leadership skills are required in order to have a successful presidency? The American system is one of checks and balances. It is a constitutional republic, not a dictatorship. In order to work within this system you have to learn the fine arts of building political capital in order to move the levers of power and get things done. It is not enough to give speeches. You have to work with your own party and, more importantly, the opposition. All successful presidents know how to do this, to one extent or another.

For example, George W Bush was able to work with Democrats to get his tax cuts, education reforms and Iraq war measures passed. Bill Clinton was able to work with a Newt Gingrich led congress to pass NAFTA, welfare reform, and balanced budgets. Ronald Reagan was able to work with the legendary Democratic House speaker Tip O'Neill to keep Social Security solvent for a quarter-century. He was able to work with liberal Democrat Bill Bradley to pass tax reform. Even the hapless Jimmy Carter was able to secure bipartisan support to get airline deregulation passed.

What are the keys to their success? The simple answer is that they've all had experience being leaders within the American system. As former governors, they learned how to work within a system of checks and balances and with people who hold views opposite to their own to get things done. It's not easy, but then the system was never designed to BE easy. It was meant to keep power diffuse. It was designed to prevent one man, especially the president, from exercising too much power.

In order to operate the levers of power it is vital for any president to build and maintain political capital. This means making time for members of congress, especially members of the opposition. Calling them up and talking to them, finding out what their needs and concerns are, this is the currency of the realm. All of the presidents above were good at this, but none more so, perhaps, than Bill Clinton.

Bill Clinton is instructive, as in many ways he is everything Obama is not. Bill Clinton leaned how to be a leader through the actual act of governing. He actually wielded executive power as a governor in Arkansas, and then learned a great deal more once he lost it. Failure is a great teacher, but you have to be willing to put yourself out there to fail in the first place.

Bill Clinton became the youngest governor in American history when he was elected at the tender age of 32. As is often the case with untested youth, he thought he knew it all. He didn't really care what anyone else thought and paid little attention to those around him. He knew best, and he attempted to steamroll any and all opposition. He tried to ram his ideas right through the American system, rather than work within it. When it came time for re-election he had no political allies and little political capital. He was defeated.

However, the seeds of his political rebirth were sown in this defeat. Bill Clinton learned you have to listen to other people, especially people from the other party. Face time with a leader is critically important. You have to make time for people as its part of the job of building political capital. It takes work, but it's the only way to get anything done.

My favorite Clinton story, and one that reveals his love and skill for this particular kind of necessary political schmoozing, is when he visited my home province of British Columbia as president. He was greeted at the airport by then Premier Glen Clark. As soon as he got off the plane, Clinton proceeded to wrap Clark around his little finger. He complimented him, told him little stories and generally made him feel like he was the most important person in the world. Clark's staff couldn't believe how giddy he was after his brief meeting with the president. Bill Clinton had reduced our tough as nails premier to that of a giddy schoolgirl. Now, did Bill Clinton need Glen Clark's vote?

Not in the least. But by that point charming potential allies and building political capital had become so common for Clinton it must have been like breathing. It was just something he did.

Barack Obama, on the other hand, has never run anything in his life except his mouth. He has no executive experience. He has never put himself out there like Bill Clinton did where he was forced to learn from bitter defeat. He never learned the value of collecting political capital or how to get things done within the American system of checks and balances. He has simply wafted higher and higher like a feather, lifted by the empty rhetoric of his own speeches. Is it any surprise then that once he gained the presidency and actually had to perform, he didn't know what to do? This is how Chris Mathews puts it:

"Their idea of running a campaign is a virtual universe of sending emails around to people. No it's not, it's meetings with people. It's forging alliances. It's White House meetings and dinner parties that go on til midnight. And he should be sitting late at night now, with senators and members of congress and governors, working together on how they're gonna win this political fight that's coming. I don't get a sense that he's ever had a meeting. I hear stories that you wouldn't believe.
not a single phone call since the election. ... They don't call. Members of congress, I keep asking, when did you hear from him last? ... he doesn't like their company."

Does this sound like someone with executive experience who knows how to get things done? Someone who doesn't call members of his own party, never mind the opposition? Can you imagine anyone talking about Bill Clinton this way? It's impossible, because Bill Clinton, as well as any successful president, knows that this is part of the job.

This view, of a person who has actual disdain for the necessary Washington ways of talking to people, listening, and building political capital, is further confirmed with this Obama comment:

"I can't believe I've got to meet with all these congressman from Podunk city to get my bills passed".

Obama reportedly has made this comment several times to world leaders. Well, you may not want to meet with that congressman from "Podunk", you may think that he or she is unimportant, but they're not. If you want to get things done in the American system you have to understand the concerns of those congressman as they represent a section of the American people. Every successful president has understood this. By all appearances, it seems that Obama does not, and has no desire to learn.

Obama's preferred style of leadership, if you can call it that, is described in an article by Ryan Lizza. Like a tenured out of touch college professor he likes to stay up late, read memos, and take notes, rather than putting in the actual work that it takes to be effective. Blogger Mickey Kaus put it this way:

"The president's decision-making method -- at least as described in this piece -- seems to consist of mainly checking boxes on memos his aides have written for him."

This may be the method that Obama prefers, but it's not a style that can work for a president, and it isn't leadership.

Just as Obama has disdain for the real political work of building political capital to get legislation passed, he is seemingly above being involved in its creation as well. For every piece of major legislation that has been passed, he has been aloof, distant, and not involved. For his health care plan, even democrats were "baffled" and "frustrated" by the lack of direction from Obama. A senior democratic congressional source had this to say to CNN:

"We appreciate the rhetoric and his willingness to ratchet up the pressure but what most Democrats on the Hill are looking for is for the president to weigh in and make decisions on outstanding issues. Instead of sending out his people and saying the president isn't ruling anything out, members would like a little bit of clarity on what he would support – especially on how to pay for his health reform bill,"

He couldn't be bothered to craft his signature near trillion-dollar stimulus program, or even participate in it. Instead, he left it to the Nancy Pelosi controlled congress to write the bill. What emerged from this process was a monstrosity so full of pork and liberal nostrums that even some Democrats voted against it.

His most spectacular demonstration of his utter lack of leadership ability is on the issue of America's budget and debt. Not only has he never proposed any ideas for entitlement reform, he has proven himself incapable of producing a budget that can garner a single Democratic vote.

When it comes to his failure to show leadership and get things done, Obama resorts to whining and blame. It's as if his gigantic ego keeps telling him that he's a great leader who gets things done. When nasty reality keeps proving him wrong, he is forced to make pathetic, un-leader like excuses. As Jonah Goldberg put it:

"It's like the guy who insists that he's a real ladies' man but can't get a phone number because all of the hot women in the bar just happen to be gay"

Typically, Obama blames what he calls a do nothing Congress. This despite the fact that he enjoyed 2 massive majorities for two years and the only reason he lost those majorities is that he was so inept the American people wanted to rein him in.

He also loves to blame his predecessor in the most undignified and un-presidential ways imaginable. Even if you are handed a mess, people elected you as a leader to clean it up. Either get on with the job, if you're able, or get out of the way. Reagan was a shining example of this. Despite inheriting an economy with inflation at 13.5 percent, the prime rate at 21 percent, and the USSR getting away with murder all over the world, Reagan was always kind to Carter in public statements. As his biographer Lou Cannon wrote:

"Reagan ... was generous to Carter in his public statements even though he did not care for him."

Reagan knew that Americans didn't wanted to hear whining about how tough his job was, they wanted to know his plan for fixing it. That's what real leaders do.

On the rare occasions when he's not whining about his inability to work with congress or blaming Bush, he will even stoop to blame the American people themselves. This is how he put it in a State of the Union message, in which he spoke of the armed forces.

"They're not consumed with personal ambition. They don't obsess over their differences . . . They work together. Imagine what we could accomplish if we followed their example."

Ok, that's nice, but what's the subtext? The reason the military works the way it does is because the men and women in uniform voluntarily accept a top down command

199

structure for the greater good. Unfortunately for Obama, however, a military unit is not a republic of free citizens. When Obama implores people to follow the military's example, he is in fact telling people to follow HIM. If only the American people would just sit down, shut up, and subsume themselves to his brilliant leadership, like they do in China, they could get so much done.

Obama is not a leader, and these are the ranting's of a man who at a very basic level does not understand what America is all about.

Towards the end of the Carter presidency there was a lot of talk about the office being unmanageable and simply too big for one man to handle. All of this talk faded away when a real leader who understood how to work the levers of power, Ronald Reagan, became leader. Charles Krauthammer put it this way:

"It turned out that the country's problems were not problems of structure but of leadership. Reagan and Clinton had it. Carter didn't. Under a president with extensive executive experience, good political skills and an ideological compass in tune with the public, the country was indeed governable."

That last sentence is key - *Under a president with extensive executive experience, good political skills, and an ideological compass in tune with the public.* Obama has none of these. He had no executive experience prior to coming into office and has shown no evidence of learning any since. His only political skills consist of giving shallow political speeches and his ideological compass isso out of tune with the majority of Americans that he is constantly forced to hide it.

For not possessing or demonstrating the leadership skills that America desperately needs at this time, Barack Obama sucks.

I, Pencil

By Leonard E. Read

I am a lead pencil—the ordinary wooden pencil familiar to all boys and girls and adults who can read and write.

Writing is both my vocation and my avocation; that's all I do.

You may wonder why I should write a genealogy. Well, to begin with, my story is interesting. And, next, I am a mystery —more so than a tree or a sunset or even a flash of lightning. But, sadly, I am taken for granted by those who use me, as if I were a mere incident and without background. This supercilious attitude relegates me to the level of the commonplace. This is a species of the grievous error in which mankind cannot too long persist without peril. For, the wise G. K. Chesterton observed, "We are perishing for want of wonder, not for want of wonders."

I, Pencil, simple though I appear to be, merit your wonder and awe, a claim I shall attempt to prove. In fact, if you can understand me—no, that's too much to ask of anyone—if you can become aware of the miraculousness which I symbolize, you can help save the freedom mankind is so unhappily losing. I have a profound lesson to teach. And I can teach this lesson better than can an automobile or an airplane or a mechanical dishwasher because—well, because I am seemingly so simple.

Simple? Yet, not a single person on the face of this earth knows how to make me. This sounds fantastic, doesn't it? Especially when it is realized that there are about one and one-half billion of my kind produced in the U.S.A. each year.

Pick me up and look me over. What do you see? Not much meets the eye—there's some wood, lacquer, the printed labeling, graphite lead, a bit of metal, and an eraser.

Innumerable Antecedents

Just as you cannot trace your family tree back very far, so is it impossible for me to name and explain all my antecedents. But I would like to suggest enough of them to impress upon you the richness and complexity of my background.

My family tree begins with what in fact is a tree, a cedar of straight grain that grows in Northern California and Oregon. Now contemplate all the saws and trucks and rope and the countless other gear used in harvesting and carting the cedar logs to the railroad siding. Think of all the persons and the numberless skills that went into their fabrication: the mining of ore, the making of steel and its refinement into saws, axes, motors; the growing of hemp and bringing it through all the stages to heavy and strong rope; the logging camps with their beds and mess halls, the cookery and the raising of all the foods. Why, untold thousands of persons had a hand in every cup of coffee the loggers drink!

The logs are shipped to a mill in San Leandro, California. Can you imagine the individuals who make flat cars and rails and railroad engines and who construct and install the communication systems incidental thereto? These legions are among my antecedents.

Consider the millwork in San Leandro. The cedar logs are cut into small, pencil-length slats less than one-fourth of an inch in thickness. These are kiln dried and then tinted for the same reason women put rouge on their faces. People prefer that I look pretty, not a pallid white. The slats are waxed and kiln dried again. How many skills went into the making of the tint and the kilns, into supplying the heat, the light and power, the belts, motors, and all the other things a mill requires? Sweepers in the mill among my ancestors? Yes, and included are the men who poured the concrete for the dam of a Pacific Gas & Electric Company hydroplant which supplies the mill's power!

Don't overlook the ancestors present and distant who have a hand in transporting sixty carloads of slats across the nation.

Once in the pencil factory—$4,000,000 in machinery and building, all capital accumulated by thrifty and saving parents of mine—each slat is given eight grooves by a complex machine, after which another machine lays leads in every other slat, applies glue, and places another slat atop—a lead sandwich, so to speak. Seven brothers and I are mechanically carved from this "wood-clinched" sandwich.

My "lead" itself—it contains no lead at all—is complex. The graphite is mined in Ceylon [Sri Lanka]. Consider these miners and those who make their many tools and the makers of the paper sacks in which the graphite is shipped and those who make the string that ties the sacks and those who put them aboard ships and those who make the ships. Even the lighthouse keepers along the way assisted in my birth—and the harbor pilots.

The graphite is mixed with clay from Mississippi in which ammonium hydroxide is used in the refining process. Then wetting agents are added such as sulfonated tallow—animal fats chemically reacted with sulfuric acid. After passing through numerous machines, the mixture finally appears as endless extrusions—as from a sausage grinder—cut to size, dried, and baked for several hours at 1,850 degrees Fahrenheit. To increase their strength and smoothness the leads are then treated with a hot mixture which includes candelilla wax from Mexico, paraffin wax, and hydrogenated natural fats.

My cedar receives six coats of lacquer. Do you know all the ingredients of lacquer? Who would think that the growers of castor beans and the refiners of castor oil are a part of it? They are. Why, even the processes by which the lacquer is made a beautiful yellow involve the skills of more persons than one can enumerate!

Observe the labeling. That's a film formed by applying heat to carbon black mixed with resins. How do you make resins and what, pray, is carbon black?

My bit of metal—the ferrule—is brass. Think of all the persons who mine zinc and copper and those who have the skills to make shiny sheet brass from these products of nature. Those black rings on my ferrule are black nickel. What is black nickel and how is it applied? The complete story of why the center of my ferrule has no black nickel on it would take pages to explain.

Then there's my crowning glory, inelegantly referred to in the trade as "the plug," the part man uses to erase the errors he makes with me. An ingredient called "factice" is what does the erasing. It is a rubber-like product made by reacting rapeseed oil from the Dutch East Indies [Indonesia] with sulfur chloride. Rubber, contrary to the common notion, is only for binding purposes. Then, too, there are numerous vulcanizing and accelerating agents. The pumice comes from Italy; and the pigment which gives "the plug" its color is cadmium sulfide.

No One Knows

Does anyone wish to challenge my earlier assertion that no single person on the face of this earth knows how to make me?

Actually, millions of human beings have had a hand in my creation, no one of whom even knows more than a very few of the others. Now, you may say that I go too far in relating the picker of a coffee berry in far-off Brazil and food growers elsewhere to my creation; that this is an extreme position. I shall stand by my claim. There isn't a single person in all these millions, including the president of the pencil company, who contributes more than a tiny, infinitesimal bit of know-how. From the standpoint of know-how the only difference between the miner of graphite in Ceylon and the logger in Oregon is in the type of know-how. Neither the miner nor the logger can be dispensed with, any more than can the chemist at the factory or the worker in the oil field— paraffin being a by-product of petroleum.

Here is an astounding fact: Neither the worker in the oil field nor the chemist nor the digger of graphite or clay nor any who mans or makes the ships or trains or trucks nor the one who runs the machine that does the knurling on my bit of metal nor the president of the company performs his singular task because he wants me. Each one wants me less, perhaps, than does a child in the first grade. Indeed, there are some among this vast multitude who never saw a pencil nor would they know how to use one. Their motivation is other than me. Perhaps it is something like this: Each of these millions sees that he can thus exchange his tiny know-how for the goods and services he needs or wants. I may or may not be among these items.

There is a fact still more astounding: The absence of a master mind, of anyone dictating or forcibly directing these countless actions which bring me into being. No trace of such a person can be found. Instead, we find the Invisible Hand at work. This is the mystery to which I earlier referred.

It has been said that "only God can make a tree." Why do we agree with this? Isn't it because we realize that we ourselves could not make one? Indeed, can we even describe a tree? We cannot, except in superficial terms. We can say, for instance, that a certain molecular configuration manifests itself as a tree. But what mind is there among men that could even record, let alone direct, the constant changes in molecules that transpire in the life span of a tree? Such a feat is utterly unthinkable!

I, Pencil, am a complex combination of miracles: a tree, zinc, copper, graphite, and so on. But to these miracles which manifest themselves in Nature an even more extraordinary miracle has been added: the configuration of creative human energies— millions of tiny know-hows configurating naturally and spontaneously in response to human necessity and desire and in the absence of any human masterminding! Since only God can make a tree, I insist that only God could make me. Man can no more direct these millions of know-hows to bring me into being than he can put molecules together to create a tree.

The above is what I meant when writing, "If you can become aware of the miraculousness which I symbolize, you can help save the freedom mankind is so unhappily losing." For, if one is aware that these know-hows will naturally, yes, automatically, arrange themselves into creative and productive patterns in response to human necessity and demand— that is, in the absence of governmental or any other coercive master-minding—then one will possess an absolutely essential ingredient for freedom: a faith in free people. Freedom is impossible without this faith.

Once government has had a monopoly of a creative activity such, for instance, as the delivery of the mails, most individuals will believe that the mails could not be efficiently delivered by men acting freely. And here is the reason: Each one acknowledges that he himself doesn't know how to do all the things incident to mail delivery. He also recognizes that no other individual could do it. These assumptions are correct. No individual possesses enough know-how to perform a nation's mail delivery any more than any individual possesses enough know-how to make a pencil. Now, in the absence of faith in free people—in the unawareness that millions of tiny know-hows would naturally and miraculously form and cooperate to satisfy this necessity—the individual cannot help but reach the erroneous conclusion that mail can be delivered only by governmental "masterminding."

Testimony Galore

If I, Pencil, were the only item that could offer testimony on what men and women can accomplish when free to try, then those with little faith would have a fair case. However, there is testimony galore; it's all about us and on every hand. Mail delivery is exceedingly simple when compared, for instance, to the making of an automobile or a calculating machine or a grain combine or a milling machine or to tens of thousands of other things. Delivery? Why, in this area where men have been left free to try, they deliver the human voice around the world in less than one second; they deliver an event visually and in motion to any person's home when it is happening; they deliver 150 passengers from Seattle to Baltimore in less than four hours; they deliver gas from Texas to one's range or furnace in New York at unbelievably low rates and without subsidy; they deliver each four pounds of oil from the Persian Gulf to our Eastern Seaboard—halfway around the world— for less money than the government charges for delivering a one-ounce letter across the street!

The lesson I have to teach is this: Leave all creative energies uninhibited. Merely organize society to act in harmony with this lesson. Let society's legal apparatus remove all obstacles the best it can. Permit these creative know-hows freely to flow. Have faith that free men and women will respond to the Invisible Hand. This faith will be confirmed. I, Pencil, seemingly simple though I am, offer the miracle of my creation as testimony that this is a practical faith, as practical as the sun, the rain, a cedar tree, the good earth.

Selected Bibliography

Introduction

Caddell, Pat. "Media Have Become 'Enemy Of The American People'". Breitbart.TV. http://www.breitbart.com/Breitbart-TV/2012/09/30/Pat-Caddell-Says-Media-Have-Become-an-Enemy-of-the-American-people (Sept 30, 2012)

Hinderaker, John. "Hurricanes, Then And Now". Powerline. http://www.powerlineblog.com/archives/2012/11/hurricanes-then-and-now.php (Nov 18, 2012)

Reason #26 - Cash for Clunkers

Chapman, Steve. "The Real Clunkers in this Deal". Real Clear Politics. http://www.realclearpolitics.com/articles/2009/08/09/the_real_clunkers_in_this_deal_97828.html (August 9, 2009)

Harrop, Froma. "Cash for Clunkers Means 'Ca-Ching' for Detroit". Real Clear Politics. http://www.realclearpolitics.com/articles/2009/08/04/cash_for_clunkers_means_ca-ching_for_detroit_97753.html (August 4, 2009)

Seelye, Katharine Q. "Dealers Race to Get Their Clunkers Crushed". <u>New York Times</u>. http://thelede.blogs.nytimes.com/2009/07/31 /dealers-race-to-get-their-clunkers-crushed/?hp
(July 31, 2009)

Stossel, John. "Cash for Clunkers". <u>Fox Business</u>. http://www.foxbusiness.com/on-air/stossel/blog/2010/07/01/cash-for-clunkers
(July 1, 2010)

Stossel, John. "Economic Illiterates In Washington". <u>Real Clear Politics</u>. http://www.realclearpolitics.com/articles/200 9/09/02/clunker_legislation_98131.html
(September 2, 2009)

"Top 20 Cash for Clunkers Quotes". <u>Car Dealer Reviews</u>. http://www.cardealerreviews.org/?p=116708
(August 23, 2009)

Reason #25 - Radically Pro-Abortion

Gerson, Michael. "Obama's Catholic Strategy in Shambles". Real Clear Politics. http://www.realclearpolitics.com/articles/201 1/11/15/obamas_catholic_strategy_in_shambl es_112067.html
(November 15, 2011)

Lowry, Rick. "Obama Lying About His Abortion Record". <u>Real Clear Politics.</u> http://www.realclearpolitics.com/articles/200 8/08/barack_obama_abortion_extremis.html

(August 19, 2008)

May, Caroline. "Obama opposes ban on sex-selective abortions". The Daily Caller. http://dailycaller.com/2012/05/31/obama-opposes-ban-on-sex-selective-abortions/ (May 5, 2012)

Stanley, Tim. "Obama's Democrats won't outlaw sex-selection abortions? The voters, China and Hillary Clinton would". The Telegraph. http://blogs.telegraph.co.uk/news/timstanley/100162067/obamas-democrats-wont-outlaw-sex-selection-abortions-the-voters-china-and-hillary-clinton-would/ (May 31, 2012)

Vance, Kevin. "Obama's Abortion Distortion". Weekly Standard. http://www.weeklystandard.com/Content/Public/Articles/000/000/015/404kfgky.asp (August 13, 2008)

Reason #24 - Eric Holder

Babbin, Jed. "Questions Holder Needs To Answer". Human Events http://www.humanevents.com/2009/01/14/questions-holder-needs-to-answer/ (January 14, 2009)

Gerson, Michael. "An Attorney General Lacking Trust". Washington Post. http://www.washingtonpost.com/opinions/michael-gerson-an-attorney-generals-want-of-trust/2012/06/25/gJQA3ZPp2V_story.html

(June 26, 2012)

Lowry, Rich. "Holder's Identity Problem". Real Clear Politics. http://www.realclearpolitics.com/articles/2012/03/13/holders_identity_problem_113463.html (March 13, 2012)

McCarthy, Andrew. "AG Holder Refuses to Say 'Radical Islam'". National Review. http://www.nationalreview.com/corner/199355/ag-eric-holder-refuses-say-radical-islam-cause-terrorism-committed-muslims-andrew-c-mc (May 13, 2010)

Mirengoff, Paul. "Undermining faith in law enforcement and national security: the legacy of Eric Holder". Powerline. http://www.powerlineblog.com/archives/2012/12/undermining-faith-in-law-enforcement-and-national-security-the-legacy-of-eric-holder.php (Dec 4, 2012)

Sowell, Thomas. "Reverse Racism". Real Clear Politics. http://www.realclearpolitics.com/articles/2011/10/11/reverse_racism_111636.html (Oct 11, 2011)

Saunders, Debra. "Obama and His New Crew". Real Clear Politics. http://www.realclearpolitics.com/articles/2008/12/obama_and_his_new_crew.html (December 4, 2008)

Pareene, Alex. "DOJ inquiry says "New Black Panther" case was handled appropriately". Salon.
http://www.salon.com/2011/03/30/black_panther_case_investigation/
(March 30, 2011)

Kobach, Kris. "A Loss for America". New York Post.
http://www.nypost.com/p/news/opinion/opedcolumnists/loss_for_america_nxkrr/XdjXIJ1ngqXVO8nL
(Nov 14, 2009)

Reason #23 - Gun Control

Edwards, Steven. "UN arms treaty could put U.S. gun owners in foreign sights, say critics". Fox News.
http://www.foxnews.com/world/2012/07/11/un-arms-treaty-could-put-us-gun-owners-in-foreign-sights-say-critics/
(July 12, 2012)

Read more:
http://www.foxnews.com/world/2012/07/11/un-arms-treaty-could-put-us-gun-owners-in-foreign-sights-say-critics/#ixzz20KueMann

Hughes, Brian. "Obama expected to push gun control in second term". Washington Examiner.
http://washingtonexaminer.com/obama-expected-to-push-gun-control-in-second-term/article/2515196#.UMI9CoXbbcY
(Dec 5, 2012)

Jacoby, Jeff. "A silver bullet for Obama?" Boston.com. http://www.boston.com/bostonglobe/editorial_opinion/oped/articles/2008/06/29/a_silver_bullet_for_obama/ (June 29, 2008)

Morris, Dick. "Obama's Secret Gun Control plan!". Youtube. http://www.youtube.com/watch?v=FmPG9oHh1aI (July 10, 2012)

Morrissey, Ed. "Obama: We're working on gun control 'under the radar'". Hot Air. http://hotair.com/archives/2011/05/25/obama-were-working-on-gun-control-under-the-radar/ (May 25, 2011)

Pavlich, Katie. "Obama's Coming Gun Control: Through the UN". Townhall. http://townhall.com/tipsheet/katiepavlich/2012/07/09/obamas_coming_gun_control_through_the_un (July 9, 2012)

Scullum, Jacob. "Revenge of the Bitter Gun Owners". Reason. http://reason.com/archives/2008/09/24/revenge-of-the-bitter-gun-owne (September 24, 2008)

"Small Arms Treaty". Snopes.com. http://www.snopes.com/politics/guns/untreaty.asp

(July 9, 2012)

Stein, Sam. "Obama Looking for Ways Around Congress On Gun Policy". <u>Huffington Post</u>. <u>http://www.huffingtonpost.com/2011/03/15/obama-gun-laws-congress_n_836138.html</u> (March 15, 2011)

Workman, Dave. "Watch out for the 'small, print' in U.N. arms trade treaty". <u>Examiner.</u> <u>http://www.examiner.com/article/watch-out-for-the small-print-u-n-arms-trade-treaty</u> (July 10, 2012)

Reason #22 - Treating Britain Poorly

Gardiner, Nile. "Barack Obama's top 10 insults against Britain". <u>The Telegraph</u>. <u>http://blogs.telegraph.co.uk/news/nilegardiner/100027838/barack-obama</u>'s-top-10-insults-against-britain/
March 1, 2010

"The Betrayal Of Great Britain". <u>Investors Daily</u>. <u>http://news.investors.com/article/562301/201102071743/the-betrayal-of-great-britain.htm</u> (February 7, 2011)

Reason #21 - The Keystone Pipeline

Baily, Ronald. "President Obama Bows to Special Interests: Refuses to Approve Keystone XL Pipeline from Canada". <u>Reason</u>. <u>http://reason.com/blog/2012/01/18/president-obama-bows-to-special-interest</u> (January 18, 2012)

"Canada's Harper talks oil with China as U.S. faces $4 gas". Washington Examiner. http://washingtonexaminer.com/opinion/edit orials/2012/02/canadas-harper-talks-oil-china-us-faces-4-gas/253826 (February 09, 2012)

Loris, Nicolas. "Obama's "Forced" Keystone Decision Rejects Jobs, Energy, and Logic". The Foundry. http://blog.heritage.org/2012/01/18/obama%E2%80%99s-forced-keystone-decision-rejects-jobs-energy-and-logic/ (January 18, 2012)

Norton, Gale. "Obama chooses American decline". Washington Times. http://www.washingtontimes.com/news/2012/jan/20/obama-chooses-american-decline/ (January 20, 2012)

Steward, Leighton H. "Voodoo Environomics". Washington Times. http://www.washingtontimes.com/news/2012/feb/17/voodoo-environomics/ (February 17, 2012)

Reason #20 - Reneging on the Missile Shield

Gardiner, Nile. "Barack Obama surrenders to Russia on Missile Defence". The Telegraph. http://blogs.telegraph.co.uk/news/nilegardiner/100010237/barack-obama-surrenders-to-russia-on-missile-defence/ (September 17, 2009)

Peters, Ralph. "Obama feeds allies to bear".
New York Post.
http://www.nypost.com/p/news/opinion/ope
dcolumnists/obama_feeds_allies_to_bear_P
MpzvTatl7WiRqyYL3ZtvJ
(September 19, 2009)

Smith, Ben. "Polish PM wouldn't take U.S.
calls". Politico.
http://www.politico.com/blogs/bensmith/090
9/Polish_PM_wouldnt_take_US_calls.html
(September 17, 2009)

Steyn, Mark. "Mark Steyn: Obama helping
Putin restitch Iron Curtain". OC Register.
http://www.ocregister.com/articles/obama-
211793-missile-defense.html
(September 18, 2009)

Reason #19 - General Motors Auto Bailout

Picket, Kerry. "Barack Obama: Losing $84
billion big success". The Washington Times.
http://www.washingtontimes.com/blog/water
cooler/2011/mar/31/barack-obama-losing-84-
billion-big-success/
(March 31, 2011)

Zywicki, Todd. "Chrysler and the Rule of Law".
Wall Street Journal.
http://online.wsj.com/article/SB12421735683
6613091.html
(May 13, 2009)

Jackson, David. "Obama on car bailout: I was betting on American workers". USA Today. http://content.usatoday.com/communities/theoval/post/2012/07/obama-on-auto-bailout-i-was-betting-on-american-worker-/1#.T_ixRXCQbcY
(June 5, 2012)

Levine, Michael. "How Washington blew GM's bankruptcy". Financial Times. http://www.ft.com/intl/cms/s/0/cd00d2c6-4ee2-11de-8c10-00144feabdc0.html#axzz1sWPPCcCK
(June 1, 2009)

Lott, John. "Obama and GM Cook the Books". National Review. http://www.nationalreview.com/articles/300075/obama-and-gm-cook-books-john-lott-jr#
(May 16, 2012)

McMorris, Bill. "The Auto Bailout Bust". FreeBeacon.com. http://freebeacon.com/the-auto-bailout-bust/print/
(April 30, 2012)

Muir, David. "GM Posts Record $7.6 Billion Dollar Profit". ABC News. http://abcnews.go.com/blogs/business/2012/02/gm-posts-record-7-6-billion-profit/
(February 16, 2012)

"Taxpayers Get Bigger Bill From GM, Chrysler Bailout". Investors Business Daily. http://news.investors.com/article/592192/201111181758/taxpayers-lose-with-gm-and-chrysler-bailout.htm

(November 18, 2011)

Reason #18 - Failed Energy Policies

"Bam's gas-price plan". New York Post. http://www.nypost.com/p/news/opinion/edit orials/bam_gas_price_plan_B1bfwSlY9X99J1 gwZYctGM
(February 23, 2012)

Harsanyi, David. "Aren't High Gas Prices What Democrats Want?". Real Clear Politics. http://www.realclearpolitics.com/articles/201 2/02/22/arent_high_gas_prices_what_demo crats_want_113206.html
(February 22, 2012)

Hinderaker, John. "More Deception on Energy From Obama". Powerline. http://www.powerlineblog.com/archives/2012 /02/more-deception-on-energy-from- obama.php
(February 23, 2012)

Holt, David. "Obama's State of the Union Energy Claims Undercut by Record". Breitbart.com. http://www.breitbart.com/Big- Government/2012/01/26/Obamas-State-of- the-Union-Energy-Claims-Undercut-by- Record
(January 26, 2012)

Noon, Marita. "Where Will You Be When the Lights Go Out?". Townhall. http://finance.townhall.com/columnists/marit anoon/2012/06/03/where_will_you_be_whe n_the_lights_go_out/page/2

(June 2, 2012)

Samuelson, Robert. "The Bias Against Oil and Gas". <u>Real Clear Politics</u>. http://www.realclearpolitics.com/articles/200 9/05/04/the_bias_against_oil_and_gas_963 24.html
(May 4, 2009)

Reason #17 - Gutting Welfare Reform

Brooks, Arthur C. "Arthur Brooks: Obama and 'Earning Your Success'". <u>Wall Street Journal</u>. http://online.wsj.com/article/SB10000872396 390444860104577558701241637894.html?mo d=WSJ_Opinion_LEADTop
(August 6, 2012)

Ellis, Diane. "Obama Puts an End to Welfare Reform". <u>Ricochet.</u> http://ricochet.com/main-feed/Obama-Puts-an-End-to-Welfare-Reform
(July 13, 2012)

Hinderaker, John. "The Rise And Fall Of Welfare Reform". <u>Powerline</u>. http://www.powerlineblog.com/archives/2012 /08/the-rise-and-fall-of-welfare-reform.php
(August 7, 2012)

Mirengoff, Paul. "Washington Post pushes Obama's bogus line on welfare reform". <u>Powerline</u>.http://www.powerlineblog.com/arc hives/2012/08/washington-post-pushes-obamas-bogus-line-on-welfare-reform.php
(August 8, 2012)

Rector, Robert. "Obama's Attack on 'Workfare'"". National Review. http://www.nationalreview.com/articles/3133 50/obama-s-attack-workfare-robert-rector (August 8, 2012)

Reason #16 - Religious Freedom and the HHS Mandate

Chapman, Steve. "Inoculating Against Religious Freedom". Real Clear Politics. http://www.rcalclearpolitics.com/articles/201 2/02/02/inoculating_against_religious_freed om_112995.html (February 2, 2012)

Hemmingway, Molly. "Massive religious liberty lawsuit, minor broadcast coverage". GetReligion.org. http://www.getreligion.org/2012/05/massive-religious-liberty-lawsuit-minor-broadcast-coverage/ (June 21, 2012)

Henninger, Daniel. "Henninger: Church Is Still Not State". Wall Street Journal. http://online.wsj.com/article/SB10001424052 7023036401045774364320651344466.html (May 30, 2012)

Hinderaker, John. "HOW MERITORIOUS ARE THE CATHOLIC LAWSUITS?". Powerline. http://www.powerlineblog.com/archives/2012 /05/how-meritorious-are-the-catholic-lawsuits.php

(May 24, 2012)

McGurn, William. "Obama Offends the
Catholic Left". Wall Street Journal.
http://online.wsj.com/article/SB10001424052
9702037185045771791102641964 98.html
(January 24, 2012)

Zoll, Rachel. "Contraception mandate outrages
religious groups". Associated Press.
http://apnews.myway.com/article/20120203/
D9SLSUPO0.html
(February 3, 2012)

Reason #15 - Solyndra and "Green Jobs"

Hayward, Steven F. "President Solyndra". The
Weekly Standard.
http://www.weeklystandard.com/articles/pres
ident-solyndra_594151.html?page=1
(Oct 3, 2011)

Hayward, Steven. "Epic Greenfail, Omnibus
Editon". Powerline.
http://www.powerlineblog.com/archives/2012
/04/epic-greenfail-omnibus-edition.php
(April 4, 2012)

"Obama's energy crisis". Chicago Tribune.
http://www.chicagotribune.com/news/opinion
/editorials/ct-edit-solyndra-
20111117,0,906162.story
(November 17, 2011)

Stone, Daniel and Clift, Eleanor. "Obama's Big
Green Mess". Newsweek.
http://www.thedailybeast.com/newsweek/201

1/10/16/obama-s-green-energy-agenda-flop.html
(Oct 17, 2011)

Reason #14 - Undermining The Supreme Court

Bock, Alan. "Alan Bock: Obama 2.0: The ultimate insider".
http://www.ocregister.com/articles/-231739--.html
(Jan 29, 2010)

Bolick, Clint. "Clint Bolick: The Supreme Court Stakes in 2012". Wall Street Journal.
http://online.wsj.com/article/SB10001424052702304141204577509250108648814.html
(July 9, 2012)

Gordon, John Steele. "Presidential CHutzpah". Contentions.
http://www.commentarymagazine.com/2012/04/03/obama-and-supreme-court-case/
(April 3, 2012)

Judge, Clark. "Intimidation in the Court: The President, the Supreme Court and the Constitution". Hugh Hewitt.
http://www.hughhewitt.com/blog/g/06a0739b-d8b6-40b8-abc8-b106781a4b2f
(April 3, 2012)

Mason, Jeff. "Obama takes a shot at Supreme Court over healthcare". Reuters.
http://www.reuters.com/article/2012/04/02/us-obama-healthcare-idUSBRE8310WP20120402

(April 2, 2012)

Sowell, Thomas. "'Empathy' Versus Law". <u>Real Clear Politics</u>. <u>http://www.realclearpolitics.com/articles/2009/05/05/empathy_versus_law_96335.html</u> (May 5, 2009)

Reason #13 - The Iranian Green Revolution

Feith, David and Weiss, Bari. "Denying the Green Revolution". <u>Wall Street Journal.</u> <u>http://online.wsj.com/article/SB10001424052748704224004574489772874564430.html</u> (October 23, 2009)

Goldberg, Jonah. "Obama's Iran Policy is Dead". <u>Real Clear Politics</u>. <u>http://www.realclearpolitics.com/articles/2009/06/24/obamas_iran_policy_is_a_bomb_97147.html</u> (June 24, 2009)

Krauthammer, Charles. "Obama Clueless on Iran". <u>Real Clear Politics</u>. <u>http://www.realclearpolitics.com/articles/2009/06/19/obama_clueless_on_iran.html</u> (June 19, 2009)

"Obama To Iran Green Revolution Dissidents: Drop Dead". <u>Investors Business Daily.</u> <u>http://news.investors.com/article/602609/201202281854/obama-ignored-iran-freedom-fighters-in-2009.htm</u> (February 28, 2012)

Reason #12 - Fast and Furious

"Fast And Furious Did Not Begin Under President Bush". Investors Business Daily. http://news.investors.com/article/615871/201206221823/fast-and-furious-different-than-wide-receiver.htm
(June 22, 2012)

Hinderaker, John. "Fast and Furious: Follow the Ideology". Powerline. http://www.powerlineblog.com/archives/2012/06/fast-and-furious-follow-the-ideology.php?utm_source=feedburner&utm_medium=feed&utm_campaign=Feed%3A+powerlineblog%2Flivefeed+%28Power+Line%29&utm_content=FaceBook
(June 22, 2012)

Hinderaker, John. "Obama's Claim of Executive Privilege: It's Frivolous". Powerline. http://www.powerlineblog.com/archives/2012/06/obamas-claim-of-executive-privilege-its-frivolous.php
(June 22, 2012)

"How Did Obama Know About 'Fast And Furious' Before Holder?". Youtube. http://www.youtube.com/watch?v=nBIWSyoe6vA
(Oct 13, 2011)

Limbaugh, David. "An Arrogant and Lawless Cover-Up". Townhall. http://townhall.com/columnists/davidlimbaugh/2012/06/22/an_arrogant_and_lawless_coverup/page/full/

(Jun 22, 2012)

Malcolm, John G. "About Time! Review Board Recommends Firings Over Operation Fast & Furious". National Review Online. http://www.nationalreview.com/corner/335144/about-time-review-board-recommends-firings-over-operation-fast-furious-john-g-malcolm#
(Dec 8, 2012)

Pavlich, Katie. "Obama's MurderGate: Fast and Furious Investigation to Continue Regardless of Contempt Vote". Townhall. http://townhall.com/columnists/katiepavlich/2012/06/20/obamas_murdergate_attorney_general_eric_holder_held_in_contempt/page/full/
(June 22, 2012)

Reason #11 - Gutting The Military

Boot, Max. "Slashing America's Defense: A Suicidal Trajectory". Commentary. http://www.commentarymagazine.com/article/slashing-americas-defense-a-suicidal-trajectory/
(January 2012)

Gaffney, Frank. "Obama's Defeatist Strategy". Townhall. http://townhall.com/columnists/frankgaffney/2012/01/11/obamas_defeatist_strategy/page/2
(January 11, 2012)

Herman, Arthur. "America's Disarmed Future". <u>National Review</u>. http://www.nationalreview.com/articles/2873 20/america-s-disarmed-future-arthur-herman (January 6, 2012)

Hewitt, Hugh. "Obama Channels Brits' retreat from Nazi Germany". The Washington Examiner". http://washingtonexaminer.com/opinion/colu mnists/2012/01/obama-channels-brits-retreat-nazi_germany/207446 (January 8, 2011)

"Obama's Indefensible Cuts". National Review. http://www.nationalreview.com/articles/2873 37/obamas-indefensible-cuts-editors (January 6, 2012)

Scarborough, Rowan. "Obama's war plan pins hopes on peace ". <u>The Washington Times</u>. http://www.washingtontimes.com/news/2012 /jan/8/obamas-war-plan-pins-hopes-on-peace/ (January 8, 2012)

Tweedie, Neil and Harding, Thomas. "Diamond Jubilee: The Queen no longer rules the waves". The Telegraph. http://www.telegraph.co.uk/news/uknews/the _queens_diamond_jubilee/9305678/Diamon d-Jubilee-The-Queen-no-longer-rules-the-waves.html (June 1, 2012)

Reason #10 - Not Leading On Afghanistan

Barone, Michael. "A War of Necessity Turns Out Not So Necessary". Real Clear Politics. http://www.realclearpolitics.com/articles/2009/10/05/a_war_of_necessity_turns_out_not_so_necessary_98571.html (October 5, 2009)

Gerson, Michael. "Obama's Fog of Ambivalence". Townhall. http://townhall.com/columnists/michaelgerson/2012/03/22/something (March 22, 2012)

Harnden, Toby, Harding, Thomas. "Bob Ainsworth criticises Barack Obama over Afghanistan". The Telegraph. http://www.telegraph.co.uk/news/uknews/defence/6646179/Bob-Ainsworth-criticises-Barack-Obama-over-Afghanistan.html (November 24, 2009)

Peters, Ralph. "Afghan agony: More troops won't help". New York Post. http://www.nypost.com/p/news/opinion/opedcolumnists/afghan_agony_more_troops_won_help_DILbepkOZbQIHAyOXRocAM (September 22, 2009)

Sanger, David E. "Charting Obama's Journey to a Shift on Afghanistan". New York Times. http://www.nytimes.com/2012/05/20/us/obamas-journey-to-reshape-afghanistan-war.html?pagewanted=all (May 19, 2012)

Steingart, Gabor. "Searching in Vain for the Obama Magic". <u>Spiegel Online</u>. <u>http://www.spiegel.de/international/world/op inion-searching-in-vain-for-the-obama-magic-a-664753.html</u>
(Dec 2, 2009)

Reason #9 – The Benghazi Scandal

Epstein, Reid J. "Obama pressed on failures at Univision forum". <u>Politico</u>. <u>http://www.politico.com/news/stories/0912/8 1470.html?hp=t1_3</u>
(September 20, 2012)

Hanson, Victor Davis. "Middle East Madness". <u>Real Clear Politics</u>. <u>http://www.realclearpolitics.com/articles/201 2/09/20/obamas_middle_east_myth-making_115512.html</u>
(September 20, 2012)

Hayes, Stephen F. "Permanent Spin". <u>Weekly Standard</u>. <u>http://www.weeklystandard.com/articles/per manent-spin_652887.html</u>
(Oct 1, 2012)

Larson, Lars. "Four Americans Died, Then The President Lied". <u>KXL.com</u>. <u>http://www.kxl.com/11/15/12/Four-Americans-Died-Then-The-President-L/landing.html?blockID=647029&feedID=107 12</u>
(November 15, 2012)

Nolte, John. "Benghazi-Gate Enters New Phase: The Cover Up Of The Cover Up". Big Peace. http://www.breitbart.com/Big-Peace/2012/11/23/Benghazi-Gate-Now-Cover-Up-Of-Cover-Up (November 23, 2012)

Peters, Ralph. "It's Not Adding Up". New York Post. http://www.nypost.com/p/news/opinion/opedcolumnists/it_not_adding_up_qmZRyBixLfsVquuzKN3H4L (November 18, 2012)

Rubio, Marco. "We still need answers on Benghazi". CNN. http://us.cnn.com/2012/11/29/opinion/rubio-benghazi/index.html?sr=sharebar_twitter (November 29, 2012)

Stephens, Bret. "Benghazi Was Obama's 3 am Call". Wall Street Journal. http://online.wsj.com/article/SB10000872396390444592404578030202508251578.html (October 2, 2012)

Wehner, Peter. "The Media's Benghazi Scandal". Commentary. http://www.commentarymagazine.com/2012/11/20/the-medias-benghazi-scandal/ (November 20, 2012)

York, Byron. "With Obama policy crumbling, White House blames movie for Mideast unrest". Washington Examiner. http://washingtonexaminer.com/with-obama-policy-crumbling-white-house-blames-movie-

for-mideast-
unrest/article/2508085#.UMe6ILbbbca
(September 15, 2012)

Reason #8 - Undermining Israel

"Feted in Gaza, Hamas leader hits out at
Israel". Reuters.
http://ca.reuters.com/article/topNews/idCAB
RE8B704R20121208?sp=true
(Dec 8, 2012)

Goodwin, Michael. "Israel's worst frenemy".
New York Post.
http://www.nypost.com/p/news/local/israel_
worst_frenemy_9eZqwbVo3liwOu2T4ishwM
(March 4, 2012)

Hinderaker, John. "Thank You, Iran!". Powerline.
http://www.powerlineblog.com/archives/2012
/11/thank-you-iran.php
(November 27, 2012)

Johnson, Scott. "The Friends Of Barack
Obama". Powerline.
http://www.powerlineblog.com/archives/2012
/05/the-friends-of-barack-obama.php
(May 30, 2012)

Kirchick, James. "Israel Betrayed". New York
Post.
http://www.nypost.com/f/print/news/opinion
/opedcolumnists/item_I5QDYNDOT74ik6Qgr
xfWNM
(June 20, 2012)

Klein, Aaron. "Obama Worked With Terrorist".
WND.com.
http://www.wnd.com/2008/02/57231/
(February 24, 2008)

Miller, David Aaron. "Bibi and Barack". LA
TImes.
http://articles.latimes.com/2012/jan/02/opini
on/la-oe-miller-bibi-barack-20120102
(January 2, 2012)

Mirengoff, Paul. "Why Did Obama Broker A
Victory For Hamas?" Powerline.
http://www.powerlineblog.com/archives/2012
/11/why-did-obama-broker-a-victory-for-
hamas.php
(November 27, 2012)

Stephens, Brett. "An Anti-Israel President".
Wall Street Journal.
http://online.wsj.com/article/SB10001424052
7023040665045763412129348944494.html
(May 24, 2011)

Reason #7 - Losing Iraq

Basile, Thomas. "Ghosts of Iraq haunt Obama
campaign". Washington Times.
www.washingtontimes.com/news/2012/jul/2/
ghosts-of-iraq-haunt-obama-campaign/
(July 2, 2012)

Krauthammer, Charles. "The 100 Year Lie".
Real Clear Politics.

http://www.realclearpolitics.com/articles/200
8/03/hoping_for_100_years.html
(March 28, 2008)

Krauthammer, Charles. "Who lost Iraq".
Washington Post.
http://www.washingtonpost.com/opinions/wh
o-lost-
iraq/2011/11/03/gIQAUcUqjM_story.html
(November 3, 2011)

Kristol, William. "The Democrats Fairy Tale".
The New York Times.
http://www.nytimes.com/2008/01/14/opinio
n/14kristol.html?_r=2&hp&oref=slogin
(January 14, 2008)

Reason #6 - The Stimulus

Anderson, Jeffrey H. "What Stimulus?" Weekly
Standard.
http://www.weeklystandard.com/articles/wha
t-stimulus_644424.html
(May 21, 2012)

Grabell, Michael. "How the $800B stimulus
failed". New York Post.
http://www.nypost.com/p/news/opinion/ope
dcolumnists/how_the_stimulus_failed_97Rl
MvRHLSLCiCf8op1iEM/0
(January 29, 2012)

Jackson, David. "Obama jokes about 'Shovel-
ready projects". USA Today.
http://content.usatoday.com/communities/th
eoval/post/2011/06/obama-jokes-about-
shovel-ready-projects/1#.T_peoXCQbcY

(June 13, 2011)

Samuelson, Robert. "The Squandered Stimulus". Real Clear Politics. http://www.realclearpolitics.com/articles/2009/07/20/the_squandered_stimulus.html (July 20, 2009)

Stein, Ben. "Politics Of Payoff". New York Post. http://www.nypost.com/p/news/opinion/opedcolumnists/item_k3YXkW0YEdwNPLF41RKR1K;jsessionid=6A30B6F459758251C07EC6ED65EF482C (January 31, 2009)

Reason #5 - Obamacare

Barone, Michael. "Obama skirts rule of law to reward pals, punish foes". Washington Examiner. http://washingtonexaminer.com/politics/2011/05/obama-skirts-rule-law-reward-pals-punish-foes/114378 (May 24, 2012)

Carnevale, Mary Lu. "Obama: 'If You Like Your Doctor, You Can Keep Your Doctor'". Wall Street Journal. http://blogs.wsj.com/washwire/2009/06/15/obama-if-you-like-your-doctor-you-can-keep-your-doctor/ (June 15, 2009)

Montopoli, Brian. "Obama:I Won't Sign A Bad Health Care Bill". CBS News. http://www.cbsnews.com/8301-503544_162-5178471-503544.html

(July 21, 2009)

Samuelson, Robert J. "The folly of Obamacare". Washington Post. http://www.washingtonpost.com/opinions/robert-samuelson-the-folly-of-obamacare/2012/06/17/gJQAf5o1jV_story.html?hpid=z6
(June 18, 2012)

Stossel, John. "Obamacare Abominations". http://townhall.com/columnists/johnstossel/2011/12/21/creators_oped
(Dec 21, 2011)

Reason TV. "3 Reasons To End Obamavare Before It Begins". Breitbart.com http://www.breitbart.com/Big-Government/2012/03/25/3-reasons-to-end-obamacare
(June 18, 2012)

Rubin, Jennifer. "Obamacare won't bend the cost curve". Washington Post. http://www.washingtonpost.com/blogs/right-turn/post/obamacare-wont-bend-the-cost-curve/2012/06/13/gJQAlgVWaV_blog.html
(June 13, 2012)

Reason #4 - Exploding The Debt

"5 Trillion and Change". Wall Street Journal. http://online.wsj.com/article/SB10001424052970204740904577195352148844134.html?mod=WSJ_Opinion_LEADTop
(February 2, 2012)

Bohan, Caren. "Obama says he's serious about tackling deficits". Reuters. http://www.reuters.com/article/2010/06/28/us-g20-obama-budget-idUSTRE65R0ON20100628 (June 27, 2010)

Hawkins, John. "5 Black Swans That Could Obliterate America's Future". Townhall. http://townhall.com/columnists/johnhawkins/2012/02/21/5_black_swans_that_could_obliterate_americas_future (Feb 21, 2012)

Klein, Philip. "Admin stops pretending it has long-term debt plan". Washington Examiner. http://washingtonexaminer.com/article/1129326 (February 16, 2012)

Knoller, Mark. "National Debt has increased more under Obama than under Bush". CBS News. http://www.cbsnews.com/8301-503544_162-57400369-503544/national-debt-has-increased-more-under-obama-than-under-bush/ (March 19, 2012)

Noonan, Peggy. "Beneath the Presidential Platitudes". Wall Street Journal. http://online.wsj.com/article/declarations.html (December 6, 2012)

Regnery, Alfred. "Obama's Fiscal Cliff And The Chicago Way". Big Government.

http://www.breitbart.com/Big-Government/2012/12/09/Obama-Fiscal-Cliff
(December 9, 2012)

Robb, Robert. "Obama's Deficits: Not His Fault?" Real Clear Politics.
http://www.realclearpolitics.com/articles/2010/02/03/obamas_deficits_arent_bushs_fault_100150.html
(February 3, 2010)

Stossel, John. "Politicians Fiddle While Fiscal Crisis Looms". Townhall.
http://townhall.com/columnists/johnstossel/2012/02/22/creators_oped
(Feb 22, 2012)

Williams, Walter. "Economic Chaos Ahead". Townhall.
http://townhall.com/columnists/walterewilliams/2012/02/08/economic_chaos_ahead/page/2
(Feb 08, 2012)

Reason #3 - He's Not Bi-Partisan

Broder, David. "McCain and Obama's Senate Clashes". Real Clear Politics.
http://www.realclearpolitics.com/articles/2008/08/mccain_and_obamas_senate_clash.html
(August 10, 2008)

Gerson, Michael. "Obama Has Been a Divider, Not a Uniter". Real Clear Politics.
http://www.realclearpolitics.com/articles/2009/04/the_polarizing_president.html

(April 8, 2009)

Gerson, Michael. "Obama's Partisan Makeover". Townhall. http://townhall.com/columnists/michaelgerson/2011/10/13/obamas_partisan_makeover/page/full/
(Oct 13, 2011)

Ignatius, David. "Obama: A Thin Record For a Bridge Builder". Real Clear Politics. http://www.realclearpolitics.com/articles/2008/03/more_evidence_of_obamas_bipart.html
(March 3, 2008)

Zernike, Kate and Zeleny, Jeff. "Obama in Senate: Star Power, Minor Role". http://www.nytimes.com/2008/03/09/us/politics/09obama.html?_r=2&pagewanted=1&ref=politics
(March 9, 2008)

Koffler, Keith. "Obama's Budget Speech Means the 2012 Campaign is ON". WhiteHouseDossier. http://www.whitehousedossier.com/2011/04/14/obamas-budget-speech-means-2012-campaign/
(April 14, 2011)

Krauthammer, Charles. "The Scapegoat Strategy". The Washington Post. http://www.washingtonpost.com/opinions/the-scapegoat-strategy/2011/10/13/gIQArNWViL_story.html
(October 13, 2011)

Wehner, Peter. "The Most Polarizing President Ever". Commentary. http://www.commentarymagazine.com/2012/01/27/obama-most-polarizing-president/ (January 27, 2012)

Reason #2 - He Is Economically Ignorant

Crovitz, Gordon L. "Gordon Crovitz: Who Really Invented the Internet?" Wall Street Journal. http://online.wsj.com/article/SB10000872396390444464304577539063008406518.html (July 22, 2012)

Ferrara, Peter. "The Worst Economic Recovery Since the Great Depression". Spectator. http://spectator.org/archives/2012/03/14/the-worst-economic-recovery-si (March 14, 2012)

Gewargis, Natalie. "Spread the Wealth". ABC News. http://abcnews.go.com/blogs/politics/2008/10/spread-the-weal/ (Oct 14, 2008)

Higgins, Heather. "Obama's Schadenfreude". Real Clear Politics. http://www.realclearpolitics.com/articles/2009/02/obamas_schadenfreude.html (February 24, 2009)

"Obama: The Private Sector Is Doing Fine". Real Clear Politics Video. http://www.realclearpolitics.com/video/2012/

06/08/obama_the_private_sector_is_doing_f
ine.html
(June 8, 2012)

Rubin, Jennifer. "Right Turn". Washington
Post.
http://www.washingtonpost.com/blogs/right-
turn/post/it-is-no-gaffe--obama-told-us-his-
economic-
theory/2012/06/11/gJQAZmeSUV_blog.html
(June 11, 2012)

Sowell, Thomas. "Socialist or Fascist".
Townhall.
http://townhall.com/columnists/thomassowel
l/2012/06/12/socialist_or_fascist
(June 12, 2012)

Reason #1 - He's Not A Leader

Babbin, Jed. "Obama's Failing Leadership".
Human Events.
http://www.humanevents.com/2009/02/23/o
bamas-failing-leadership/
(February 23, 2009)

Barone, Michael. "Box-Checking Obama in a
Liberal Cocoon". Real Clear Politics.
http://www.realclearpolitics.com/articles/201
2/02/06/box-
checking_obama_in_a_liberal_cocoon_11302
7.html
(February 6, 2012)

Bash, Dana. "Senator: Democrats 'baffled' by
president's health care stance". CNN.
http://politicalticker.blogs.cnn.com/2009/07/

21/senator-democrats-baffled-by-presidents-health-care-stance/
(July 21, 2009)

Charen, Mona. "Does Obama Listen to Himself?". Real Clear Politics.
http://www.realclearpolitics.com/articles/2009/12/04/does_obama_listen_to_himself_99405.html
(December 4, 2009)

Goldberg, Jonah. "Obama's Cynicism for Me, Not for Thee". National Review.
http://www.nationalreview.com/articles/291284/obama-s-cynicism-me-not-thee-jonah-goldberg
(February 17, 2012)

Krauthammer, Charles. "Call Obama's bluff". Washington Post.
http://www.washingtonpost.com/opinions/call-his-bluff/2011/07/14/gIQAfzFyEI_story.html?hpid=z4
(July 14, 2011)

Krauthammer, Charles. "Excuses for Obama's Failure to Lead". Real Clear Politics.
http://www.realclearpolitics.com/articles/2010/02/19/debunking_liberal_excuses.html
(February 19, 2010)

Smith, Kyle. "Obamalaise". New York Post.http://www.nypost.com/p/news/opinion/opedcolumnists/obamalaise_1MVxkFhreLzcohyi8RGRqJ
(March 11, 2012)

About The Author

David Nordmark is a blogger and author who has long held an interest in politics, economics and fitness. With regard to politics and economics his writing and thoughts can be found at www.davidnordmark.com. For his take on fitness-related matters visit www.animal-kingdom-workouts.com. He currently lives in Vancouver, British Columbia, Canada.

17470813R00139

Made in the USA
San Bernardino, CA
11 December 2014